Caribbean Cruises for 1st Timers

Expert Tips on Ports of Call, Best Excursions,
When to Go and More

By Scott S. Bateman

Promise Media

© 2019 by Promise Media LLC

ISBN: 9781072515319

Edition 2

Table of Contents

Preface

After more than 15 trips throughout the Caribbean, my wife and I have learned quite a bit about how to plan for a trip.

For people who have never gone before, going to the Caribbean is not quite as simple as planning a trip to Myrtle Beach or California. The number and variety of islands as well as the quirks of nature make it more complicated.

Then there are decisions about whether to take a cruise or just visit one island for a week. Do we take the kids? If so, what are the best islands for families?

And how about those big hurricanes we hear about on TV?

Personally, I wasn't too keen about taking a cruise the first time my wife suggested it to me. A half dozen cruises later, I'm quite keen about them. But again, going on the best possible cruise at the best possible time takes some planning.

We have made some mistakes along the way, but the remarkable planning expert I married plus my own background as a professional journalist and researcher helped us make a lot more good decisions than bad ones.

I hope you find my tips and experience helpful as you plan your first vacation to the Caribbean.

Caribbean Cruise Tips for 1st Timers

Planning to go on a Caribbean cruise for the first time is complicated in many ways.

Should we go on a western, eastern or southern Caribbean cruise? When is the best time to go for weather? What will it cost? How long should we go? Should we go on expensive shore excursions? If so, which ones?

Which cruise line should we take? Should we get an expensive ship cabin with a balcony or a budget-wise interior cabin?

Getting good answers to these questions is important because a wrong decision could lead to a frustrating vacation costing thousands of dollars. After more than 15 trips throughout the Caribbean, we think we have found some good answers.

Best Cruise Destinations

Cruise lines usually divide Caribbean cruises into three major regions: western, eastern and southern.

Western destinations include such major islands as Jamaica, Cozumel and Grand Cayman. They sometimes include secondary destinations such as the island of Roatan and Costa Maya on the Mexican coast.

Some of them also go to Central American countries such as Belize, Costa Rica and Panama. Cruises that leave from eastern Florida ports often stop in the Bahamas.

Western destinations have some of the best excursions including Stingray City at Grand Cayman, Dunn's River Falls in Jamaica and cave tubing in Belize.

Eastern cruises offer a wider variety of islands to visit. They include Antigua, Barbados, Dominica, Dominican Republic, Martinique, Puerto Rico, St. Kitty, St. Lucia, St. Maarten, Turks and Caicos, and the U.S. and British Virgin Islands. Again, ships disembarking from Florida may visit the Bahamas as well.

Southern cruises have the advantage with weather, especially during winter months. Those destinations are often warmer and drier, especially Aruba, Bonaire and Curacao. Southern cruises often include some of the eastern islands as well. Ships often disembark from San Juan, Puerto Rico.

Time of year is a big factor in which one to choose. Western is best during early spring, eastern is good from early spring to early summer, and southern is ideal during the winter and spring.

Best Times to Go

But what about summer and fall? The annual Caribbean hurricane season is a major factor in planning summer and fall cruises.

The hurricane season officially begins June 1 and ends Nov. 30. But June and November rarely get hurricanes and tropical storms. The season gets more active in July and climbs until reaching the high point in September and early October. Those two months have the most rainfall, tropical storms and hurricanes.

Those months are the worst times to go on a Caribbean cruise. But it doesn't stop some people from going then. They may live near the embarkation ports and can drive there for last-minute cruises if they see the weather forecast looks good for the week ahead.

People who live farther away, want to cruise in the summer and can't buy airline tickets at the last minute -- which is usually when they are most expensive -- should plan instead to cruise in early summer. The risk of rain is lower.

Western cruises are most popular from December through April because it is a dry season for many of the western destinations.

What Will It Cost?

The cost of a Caribbean cruise depends on seven big factors:

1. The length of the cruise.
2. The cruise line.
3. The available cabins.
4. The location of the ship cabin.
5. The number and cost for excursions.
6. Purchases on shore.

The most basic decision for a cruise planner is choosing the number of days to go on the cruise. For example, the most common cruise is six to nine nights long. Other cruises are as short as three to five nights and some go more than two weeks.

A simple calculation helps cruise planners with comparing prices. Simply divide the total cost by the number of nights to get a cost per night. Use that number to compare cruises with a different number of nights.

Still, seven-night cruises are especially common. Someone might do extensive searches on major travel websites, see a long list of seven-night cruises and find a wide variety of prices. Why do they vary so much even for the same number of nights?

The prices in those cases depend on the cruise line and the availability of cabins. Disney Cruise Line is often one of the most expensive. Carnival and Norwegian are among the least expensive. Their costs depend largely on the quality of food, entertainment and amenities.

Cabin costs fluctuate over a period of many months depending on how many are available. The price of the same cabin can be quite high six months before the cruise and much lower six days before the cruise if it's still available. Cruise lines don't like empty cabins.

The size and location of the cabin also is a major factor in prices. Cabins range from tiny interior cabins with no windows to massive three-bedroom suites with large balconies.

Smart shoppers will first choose their cabin size and location. Then they will watch cabin prices over a period of at least weeks if not months until the right price comes along.

The final costs come along on the cruise itself. Cruise lines try their best to get passengers to spend money on the ships and buy everything from artwork to jewelry, liquor, clothing and spa treatments.

In port, passenger discover many more ways to spend money, especially shopping and shore excursions.

Cruise planners may find it will help to start with a budget such as $1,000 per person. Subtract the essential cruise costs such as the cruise price (plus fees and port taxes). Whatever is left can go to on board and on shore expenses.

Tips for Having a Blast

Our favorite Caribbean cruise tips are lessons learned from many vacations in the region. Here are some of those lessons.

Eastern, Western or Southern?

Caribbean cruises are usually divided into eastern, western and southern cruises.

We have been on all three, the shipboard experiences are similar and the off ship experiences are not. Know your islands and especially the cruise ports before you choose which region to visit.

Some islands are lush and have great rainforests and plenty of palm trees because of heavy annual rains while others are arid and have little vegetation.

Most of the islands are former English, Dutch, Spanish and French colonies. As a result, they are much different in look, culture and atmosphere.

Most importantly, understand what you might enjoy the most and then pick the islands and the region to fit those interests -- excursions, recreation, shopping, eco-tourism, culture and history are all major attractions on the islands.

Aboard Ship

The food is everywhere, generally decent and demanding that you gain weight. Wear dress clothes on captain's night. Expect to leave the casinos with less money than you had going into them.

The quality of the shows is reflected in the price levels of each cruise line. The cafeteria food lines for breakfast and lunch are usually lengthy; go at odd times or head toward the back of the ship to see if there is another food bar that is less obvious and used.

Keep in mind:

- Get a cheap interior cabin if you plan to enjoy the onboard amenities.
- Get a more expensive cabin if you work on vacation.
- Reading and sleeping on deck are far more popular than swimming in the small, crowded pools.
- Even if you are not feeling sociable, try the formal dining at least once.

Great Excursions

Virtually all of the islands have similar duty-free shopping, nice white beaches, the usual list of water recreational activities such as diving, snorkeling, parasailing, etc.

What makes each island different is the people, the landscape and especially the unique excursions -- such as Stingray City in Cayman, Old San Juan in Puerto Rico, underwater river tubing in Belize and other adventures.

Here are some of the best excursions broken down by destination:

Eastern
- Old San Juan, Puerto Rico

- Dunn's River Falls in Jamaica
- Stingray City at Grand Cayman

Western
- Snorkeling and diving, especially in Roatan, Cozumel and Belize
- Mayan ruins on the east coast of Mexico and Central America
- Cave tubing in Belize
- Ziplining in Costa Rica

Southern
- Shipwreck scuba diving in Aruba
- Shopping in Philipsburg, St. Maarten
- Snorkeling with sea turtles in Barbados

Weather / When to Go

Cruise weather is a potential risk because of the annual hurricane season, but it's less of a risk on a cruise than if you visit one island for a week-long stopover.

The season, which of course includes frequent but less severe tropical storms, generally lasts from July to November with September being one of the worst months. If you have children to take, your options are generally limited to summers, Christmas and spring break.

Three of our cruises were during the summer, and the ship's captain avoided bad weather every time. If you don't have children, go any other time because the temperatures are still just as good and the prices are lower.

Finding a Good Deal

Plan far in advance to lock in lower prices if your time frame is limited because of family and work schedules. Shop at the last minute for fire sales if you can go on your vacation with short notice at any time of the year.

Go to the cruise Web sites and click on links that might say something like Specials. Or do what our family's cruise expert did, which was go to every cruise, travel and vacation Web site repeatedly to look for price breaks and get to know all of the prices as thoroughly as any travel agent.

Cruise prices vary based on time of year, islands visited, sellout rate and other factors. One cruise line offered an eight-day cruise to the Mexican Riviera for $769 and offered the same cruise two weeks later for only $529 or a 31 percent discount.

Here are 10 rules for shopping for a good cruise deal:

1. Start shopping months in advance
2. Prices are per person
3. When kids are out of school, prices go up
4. When weather is bad (fall months), prices go down
5. Check prices weekly to look for special promotions
6. Be aware that some cruise lines sell days and other sell nights, i.e., a seven-day cruise versus a seven-night cruise
7. Analyze prices on a per-night basis
8. Shorter cruises cost more per night, longer ones cost less
9. Look for rate cuts for ages 55+, past guests and even per state
10. Check for extra fees and surcharges

How to Book a Cruise and Save Money

Booking a cruise is easy. Booking a cruise at a great price is harder. It takes time, effort and patience.

People who have been on multiple cruises can book them easily and know intuitively when and how to go.

The process of planning and booking a cruise can be intimidating for first-timers. The following tips will make it all much easier.

1) Time of Year

Deciding when to go is the most important part of all because the time of year determines the location, cruise lines and especially the price.

For example, few people would recommend a Caribbean cruise in September because that month is the high point of the Caribbean hurricane season.

South America may be south of the U.S. and Canada, but it is winter in South America at the same time it is summer in North America. Summer for North Americans is a bad time to take a cruise in South America.

If the time of year is important because of children in school or work schedules, choosing when to go is limited and as a result there are fewer options for where to go. If there are no such restrictions, the options are wide open.

2) Length

When to go is related to the length of the cruise. Some cruises, such as

Florida to the Bahamas, may last only three days. Others that go around the world last for months.

But the most common length is usually around seven days and six nights with some a little longer and others a little shorter.

The length of the cruise also is a factor in how much it will ultimately cost. A great way to figure out the value is by dividing the total price by the number of days or nights. More often than not, a shorter cruise will cost more on a per-day basis, so longer cruises typically are a better value.

3) Itinerary

When decisions have been made on the time of year and approximate length of the cruise, it's time to look at where to go.

Northern Hemisphere cruises of course are most popular during the summer, but they also tend to be more expensive then for the same reason. Better prices often are available in the spring and drop in the fall in the Caribbean because of the hurricane season.
Western Caribbean cruises are usually more popular in the spring, while eastern Caribbean cruises are more popular during the summer.

Alaskan cruises are most common from late spring to early fall. Mediterranean cruises also are popular during the summer, but they can suffer from high temperatures and heavy crowds. Again, late spring and early fall are better times for a combination of price and moderate temperatures.

4) Cruise Line

What are the best cruise lines? There is no easy answer to that common question because all of the major cruise lines try to find a niche based on price and amenities.

Carnival Cruises is the most popular cruise line, but it is largely the result of having lower prices and fewer amenities than, say, Royal Caribbean.

Instead of worrying about which cruise line is best, focus instead on setting a budget and finding a cruise line and itinerary that fits the budget.

5) Ship

It is no exaggeration to say that some people cruise dozens and even hundreds of times in their lifetimes, and these people develop a great knowledge about individual ships.

First time cruises should not be as concerned about which ship to take with possibly one exception.

It does make sense to see what each ship for a particular cruise line and itinerary have to offer for entertainment while on board ship. Some offer unique experiences such as a climbing wall or wave pool while others do not. But keep in mind that ships with special amenities tend to be newer and have higher prices.

6) Cabin

Choosing a cabin is the next step in the process of planning a cruise, and for some people it is extremely important and for others not important at all.

The price of a cabin within a particular ship and on a particular cruise is mostly based on its size and location.

Four typical sizes or types of cabins are interior, ocean view, balcony or suite with each type costing more.

Because ships have multiple levels, the higher the level of the cabin, the higher the price. Likewise, the lower the level, the lower the price.

Cruises on on a tight budget will want to get an interior cabin on a lower level for the best possible price.

7) Amenities

Most major cruise lines offer pools (usually small ones), libraries, casinos, theaters, snack bars, shops, restaurants and other common amenities.

What really stands out from one to the other is the entertainment and the quality of the food, both of which are reflected in the price.

The less expensive cruise lines will have entertainment that is mostly provided on ship by cruise employees. Better cruise lines will often bring in professional entertainment.

Likewise, the better cruise lines will offer great food, especially at dinner, but nearly all of them offer restaurant-quality meals.

8) Excursions

Cruise ships have plenty to do on board, but it's the destinations and especially the excursions that often are the most memorable part of cruises.

Docking at a Caribbean island usually involves: a) walking into town to shop; b) finding a good place to eat; and c) doing something fun with the remaining time.

Cruise lines offer planned excursions for every port for an extra fee. Some of the excursions are routine, such as touring a town or island with a guide, while others are more extreme, such as climbing a volcano, snorkeling among reefs or swimming with sea creatures.

When getting ready to book the cruise, take a few minutes to see what excursions the ship offers and note the appeal. Some aren't worth the money while others can generate lifetime memories.

9) Vendor

Cruises can be booked three ways online:

- The cruise Web site such as Norwegian, Carnival, Royal Caribbean, Princess and Celebrity.
- A general travel site such as Expedia, Priceline and Travelocity.
- A cruise specialty site.

If the itinerary and dates are set, do visit multiple sites as early as possible and track them for what they have to offer.

Don't hesitate to call them and ask questions. They are eager to sell, and so they will be eager to offer help and information.

10) Price

Anyone who has followed most or all of the previous nine steps will find that booking a cruise based on a fair price will be much easier as a result.

Visiting any of the booking options on a regular basis will make it clear that prices change frequently depending on supply and demand.

Another factor in pricing may be a difference simply in one week to the next, so it is helpful to have at least a little flexibility on the time to go.

Finally, keep in mind that early bookers often will find good deals, but last-minute bookers may find even better ones.

To get a better sense of timing, look at some cruises that will take place within a matter of weeks and compare their prices to other cruises going to the same location months or even more than a year ahead.

Best Times to Go On a Caribbean Cruise

The best time to cruise to the Caribbean depends on personal preferences for weather, prices and crowds.

The weather is a major factor because rainfall is historically quite heavy in the Caribbean during certain times of the year.

It is especially true during the Caribbean hurricane season, which lasts from the beginning of June to the end of November. During that period, total rainfall rises until it reaches a high point in September and October. As a result, both months are the least popular times of the year to vacation in the Caribbean.

Temperatures also are a factor to consider. People who love beaches may find that winter in the Caribbean brings cooler seawater, especially in more northern destinations.

During the summer, people who don't like humidity and temperatures higher than 90 degrees Fahrenheit will find some destinations uncomfortably hot.

The most popular times to cruise, such as spring break and summer break from schools, usually have higher cruise prices and more crowded cruise ports. Couples or singles without families should avoid those times.

Each cruise season during the year has a different combination of weather, prices and crowds.

Winter Cruises

Many destinations experience a high point of tourism from December through February because of people fleeing the northern winters. But that period also has the lowest average temperatures for the Caribbean, especially in the islands lying closest to the United States.

The Bahamas remain popular because they are easy to reach from the U.S., they are a common stop for Caribbean cruises and because they are a popular golf destination.

But they also have the lowest temperatures of any islands in the Caribbean region. Seawater is usually too chilly for swimming.

Southern Caribbean cruises are a good choice during the early winter because they reach the destinations with the warmest temperatures, such as Aruba, Curacao, Panama, Costa Rica, and Cartagena Colombia.

Many of them embark from San Juan, Puerto Rico.

Western cruises also become popular in the later part of winter because they go to places that usually have a dry season combined with warmer temperatures. They include Jamaica, Grand Cayman, Cozumel, Costa Maya and Belize.

Tip: Early winter cruises are best for people who want to escape winters but worst for people who want warm temperatures for swimming. Late winter cruises are best for the western Caribbean.

Spring Cruises

As weather gets warmer, eastern Caribbean cruises start to become a better choice. Many eastern cruises begin in Florida and include the Bahamas as a port of call. The Bahamas and the nearby Turks and Caicos islands are among the coolest in the region during the winter.

The Bahamas have average high temperatures in the upper 70s Fahrenheit or mid 20s Celsius from January through March. Nassau is still a good one-day stop for its attractions, but a Bahamas-only cruise is not a good choice during this time of year for beach goers.

Other destinations do better, especially in late spring. Popular cruise islands such as St. Maarten have average high temperatures rise into the upper 80s Fahrenheit or more than 30 degrees Celsius.

Tip: Early spring is still best for warmth in the western and southern Caribbean. Late spring is a better time for eastern cruise visitors who like spending time on the beach and in the water.

Summer Cruises

The words "summer cruise in the Caribbean" may bring visions of warm weather and frolicking in the waves. But it's also a time of high heat and humidity for some islands as well as increasing rainfall for others.

Aruba, Cozumel, Grand Cayman and St. Thomas often have average high temperatures of more than 90 degrees during the day. The heat can make time on the beaches or shopping in the cruise ports uncomfortably hot. Recreational land activities on arid islands such as Aruba are even more uncomfortable.

Dominican Republic and Turks and Caicos have milder temperatures.

Summer also is a popular time to cruise for families because children have a summer break from school. The risk of rainfall rises as the summer advances, so anyone planning a cruise will find that early summer has a lower chance of rain in many destinations than later summer.

Tip: Summer cruises are best for people who love heat and worst for people who like moderate humidity and temperatures.

Fall Cruises

Cruise activity takes a big drop in September during the most active month of the hurricane season. It then begins to climb in October and November as weather becomes cooler up north and average rainfall begins to lessen.

Many destinations still have above average rainfall during October and November, which makes late fall a risky time to cruise. Anyone who considers going during the late fall may find that cruise prices are lower than average because of lower demand.

It also is a good time of year to look for a last-minute cruise deal if the seven- or 10-day weather forecast shows a low chance of rain.

Recommendation: Fall cruises are best for people looking for great deals but the worst time for rain.

Travel Insurance: Just in Case of Hurricanes

All of our baggage arrived at the cruise ship -- except for the one with all of the clothes for our son. The ship left the harbor before we could track down the taxi that still had his bag.

Our visit to St. Kitts was interrupted by my sudden tooth infection. After a great deal of pain and trouble, we located one of only two part-time dentists on the island.

These are only two real scenarios where cruise travel insurance would have helped us. But does that mean anyone going on a cruise should buy it?

Cruise travel insurance is available from many cruise lines, travel vendors such as Expedia and Travelocity, retailers such as Costco, as well as directly from insurance providers such as Allianz and TravelGuard.

In many cases, the cruise lines and vendors provide the insurance from the same company -- Stonebridge Casualty Insurance Company in Plano Texas.

Types of Coverage

In many cases, they also provide the same types of coverage:

- Flight assistance if a flight is delayed and another one is needed.
- Lost baggage for that taxi that drives away without unloading it.
- Emergency cash if a wallet is lost or stolen.
- Trip interruption or cancellation in the case of a Caribbean hurricane.
- Medical expenses when that tooth erupts into an infection on a far

off island. Even worse, a serious medical emergency may require airlifting off a cruise ship to the nearest hospital.

- Emergency evacuation when a ship runs aground, has a fire or some other accident.
- Involuntary job loss when the company hits the traveler with a layoff right before the start of the trip.
- War or terrorism in what would be a worst case scenario for a cruise ship in the wrong place at the wrong time.
- Financial default by the travel provider.

Cruise lines such as Royal Caribbean also provide complete cancellation coverage for people who might have the slightest doubt about whether they will be able to go on their trip.

The RC policy waives the non-refundable cancellation penalties and refunds the entire cost of the tickets in cash if the traveler needs to cancel for a specified reason. For any other reason, RC will provide a 75 percent credit for future cruises.

Cruise Insurance Examples

In addition to the cancellation program, Royal Caribbean offers a basic cruise insurance program that includes:

- Trip delays provides coverage up to $500 per person.
- Accident and sickness medical expenses coverage up to $10,000 per person.
- Emergency medical evacuations (to the nearest hospital) and repatriations (back to the home country) provides coverage up to $25,000 per person.
- Lost, stolen or damaged baggage coverage up to $1,500.
- Baggage delay coverage up to $500

- Carnival offers the same cancellation program as Royal Caribbean that provides a 100 percent refund for "specified reasons" and a 75 percent credit for "any other reason."

Carnival's base program includes:

- In the case of a trip delay, reimbursement of up to $500 for additional accommodations, meals and "catch-up" transportation expenses for anyone who misses the cruise departure because of carrier-caused delays or other specified reasons.
- Up to $1,500 for baggage or personal property that is lost or damaged and $500 to buy "necessary personal effects" if bags are delayed or misdirected by a common carrier for more than 24 hours.
- Up to $10,000 for medical expenses related to an illness or up to $10,000 for expenses related to an injury.
- Up to $30,000 in covered medical services and supplies (coordinated by a 24-hour assistance provider) to help ensure safe transport in case of a serious illness or injury that requires air or ground transportation back home or to a specialized facility.

Insurance Costs

Costs vary greatly depending on the length of the trip, the amount of coverage and other factors. But many policies start for less than $50.

For example, the Norwegian Cruise Line BookSafe Travel Protection Plan is available starting at $29 per person, depending on the amount of fare paid for the cruise.

TravelGuard.com has a quick and easy quote service. It requires three basic pieces of information:

- Destination country
- Departure date
- Return date
- Trip cost for each traveler
- Birth date of each traveler

The company provides several plans with different levels of coverage. The Silver Plan includes:

- 100% trip cost, cancellation or interruption
- $500 for trip Interruption (return air only)
- $500 for trip delay
- $750 for baggage and personal effects
- $200 for baggage delay
- $15,000 for accident or sickness medical expenses

An example of a trip to Barbados using the Silver Plan had a start date of Oct. 19, an end date of Oct. 26 and a deposit date of June 1. The travellers were two people ages 58 and 56.

The quote including $7 in fees was $129 or $64.50 per person. It did not include an emergency evacuation upgrade ($8 more), renters collision or flight protection ($18 more).

Changing the ages, travel dates or trip costs to a lower amount did not change the premium. Increasing the trip cost did increase the premiums.

Shop Around for Suitable Policies

Whether or not to buy cruise insurance comes down to personal considerations for many people including medical condition, job situation, a simple sense of security, the time of year and threat of bad weather.

It pays first to identify the basic types of coverage that are most desirable and then compare the numerous available plans to find the best one.

How to Save Money With Shore Excursions

Cruises offer tourists a seemingly endless amount of entertainment while on the water, causing many passengers to forget they are even at sea.

Shore excursions can seem equally packed and somewhat daunting, with masses of brochures and activities from which to choose.

The cruise line excursions are rarely included in the cruise's price. They can add a big tab to the bill at the end of the trip. Some of the more popular excursions cost up to $200 per person.

With a family of four, it's entirely possible to spend more money on a single excursion than the cost of one cruise line ticket.

Keep in mind that cruisers can do some activities for free and don't need the cruise line or a tour operator to make it happen.

For example, beach visits are often included among excursion options. But some cruise ports such as Philipsburg on St. Maarten have a beach within walking distance of the cruise terminal.

Here are four ways to lower the cost of the final excursion bill and still ensure that the trips on land are fun, exciting, and worthwhile.

1. Start By Picking 1 Excursion

At every port of call, there are a wide range of possible excursions, ranging from jet skiing, to snorkeling, to visiting ancient ruins.

Picking just one or even a few seem daunting when some ports have dozens of excursions from which to choose.

Start by picking the one excursion that everyone will enjoy the most. After taking the next step below, consider whether to add any more.

2. Set a Budget for All Excursions

Don't just set a budget for excursions. Set the budget BEFORE going on the trip.

Making such decisions while on the trip is like shopping for groceries while hungry. It may lead to temptations that drive up the total cost and result in big regrets later.

Once the budget is set, take some time to look up the costs of each excursion on your excursion shopping list. First check the prices on the cruise line Web site and then search for the local operators that provide the exact same excursions.

3. When Possible, Go Local

Cruise lines often charge high rates for their excursions because they are also providing ease, accessibility and reliability. Sometimes, this is exactly what the traveler is looking for, and they are willing to pay for it.

They also have to pass on part of their rates to the local operators that provide the excursions. The cruise line profits from the difference.

People willing to venture out will often times find more adventure and lower prices in the local options.

Travelers wanting to rent bicycles can usually find a cheaper bike rental shop than the ship's offering if they walk just a little bit farther inland after reaching shore -- or if they already know the price and location of the rental shop if they do their research before going on the cruise..

Tourists wishing to visit a monument, museum or historical landmark also can find cheaper taxis or buses to take them to their destination if they know where they want to go and are willing to research the rates for local transportation.

Cruises usually offer a snorkeling excursion, but snorkeling gear can almost always be rented locally from the public beaches, and usually at a much cheaper price.

4. Check for Last-Minute Deals

Some excursion operators offer discounts and special deals. They often are available for brief periods of time and show up on their Web sites unannounced.

It pays to bookmark those sites and keep returning to look for discounts. For example, Dolphin Discovery is the largest operator of swimming with the dolphins facilities in the Caribbean.

It recently offered a two for the price of one discount that was available for only three days. The terms:

- This offer is valid until September 23rd and you can choose the date of your swim.

- Valid for our Dolphin Encounter, Dolphin Swim Adventure and Dolphin Royal Swim programs.
- Valid when booking 7 days in advance.

The fact that the discount was offered in September raises an important point about saving money on excursions. Deals are more likely to be available during less popular months for Caribbean vacations such as September and less likely during more popular months. The most expensive dolphin deal is $199. For a family a four, a 50 percent discount will save $400.

So anyone who likes doing excursions and wants to keep their costs down may want to take their vacation during months when discounts are more likely.

What to Pack for a Caribbean Cruise

Less is usually better when deciding what to pack for a Caribbean cruise. Less is better for two reasons. One is that cruise cabins for most people are small. The more stuff, the less room.

Keep in mind as well that people often buy stuff when visiting cruise ports. They will add to the feeling of a cramped cabin and make bringing everything home a bigger challenge.

The other is a growing practice in the cruise industry -- self-assisted luggage.

With self-assisted luggage, cruisers can carry on and take off their luggage without the involvement of porters. It's especially useful for cruisers who have a few light bags and want to leave the ship as early or easily as possible.

It doesn't matter much when getting on the ship. It matters a lot more in getting off.

Anyone who has spent up to an hour looking at hundreds of baggages to find their own will attest to the frustration.

Clothes to Pack

For the first day of the cruise, pack a small carry-on bag with your travel documents, a change of clothes, bathing suit and any medications you may need. That way you don't have to wait for your checked bags to arrive in your stateroom. That said, checked bags usually arrive quickly.

For the week, think of clothing in four kinds of dining environments depending on the cruise line (some have higher standards than others) and personal preferences:

- Relaxed
- Casual
- Smart casual
- Formal

Relaxed includes shorts, T-shirts, golf shirts and tennis shoes. This style of dress is common for breakfast and lunch. It is usually acceptable in the buffet dining rooms. It also is acceptable throughout most of the ship. It is not acceptable in the full-service restaurants.

Casual, smart casual and formal are the choices for the full-service restaurants, which are optional for all guests but also popular for the higher-quality foot and even the entertainment.

Casual is the most common dress for most nights. Smart casual and formal are announced in advance.

Casual clothes generally include sport shirts and slacks for men, and sundresses or pants for women.

Smart casual means jackets and ties for men, dresses or pantsuits for women.

Formal is suits and ties or tuxedos for men, cocktail dresses for women. Whether even to bring formal clothing depends on the cruise line and whether it is low, medium or high end in pricing and clientele.

Some cruisers opt to bring casual clothes but not smart casual or formal for the sake of keeping luggage simple.

Quick tip: Pack just two or three pairs of shorts and match them with six or eight shirts. This ultra lightweight packing works best for people who don't mind eating dinner in the self-service buffet restaurants.

Other Items to Bring

- Bathing suit
- Books
- Camera
- Personal grooming items
- Workout clothes (if you are motivated)
- Hat and sunscreen

Light jackets are a good idea for winter cruises, even in the Caribbean.

The rules vary among the cruise lines when it comes to bringing alcohol on board. At the time of this writing, Carnival allowed one bottle of wine per passenger and charged a fee for the privilege. Royal Caribbean does not allow any alcohol to be brought on board.

Anything bought in duty-free areas will be stored by the ship and returned at the end of the cruise.

Do You Need a Passport?

Whether you need a passport for a cruise depends on whether you are taking a closed-loop or open-loop cruise.

A closed-loop cruise begins and ends in the same U.S. port. An open-loop cruise begins in one port and ends in another. Most cruises are closed loop.

People taking a cruise that begins and ends at the same U.S. port are usually not required to have a passport.

However, they will need proof of citizenship such as an original or certified copy of a birth certificate, a certificate of naturalization, a passport card, an enhanced driver's license (EDL) as well as a government-issued photo ID.

Children are also required to bring proof of citizenship, and if 16 and over, a photo ID is also required.

The only identification needed when getting off and on a ship at a port of call is the cruise ship ID card. Every passenger receives one after boarding for the first time.

Official Definition

U.S. Customs and Border Protection explains what documentation passengers need when they start and end a cruise.

"U.S. citizens on closed-loop cruises will be able to enter or depart the country with proof of citizenship, such as an Enhanced Driver's License (EDL), a government-issued birth certificate (issued by the Vital Records Department in the state where he or she was born) or passport, and if 16 or older, a government issued driver's license, picture ID, denoting photo, name and date of birth."

The Department of Homeland Security says:

"U.S. citizens on closed-loop cruises (cruises that begin and end at the same U.S. port) are able to enter the United States with a birth certificate and government-issued photo ID. Please be aware that you may still be required to present a passport to enter the countries your cruise ship is visiting. Check with your cruise line to ensure you have the appropriate documents."

A valid passport may not be required for a U.S. citizen taking a closed-loop cruise. But the U.S. State department and cruise lines strongly recommend that anyone taking a cruise of any kind travel with a passport

Examples of why it is important to have a passport is the possibility of missing the scheduled embarkation from a port or disembarking the ship in case of an emergency. We witnessed such a situation on our most recent eastern Caribbean cruise when an elderly passenger left the ship by helicopter to go to a hospital on a nearby island.

Cruise travelers in those situations will need their passports to use the local airport to fly back to the U.S.

Regardless, anyone taking a cruise needs proof of citizenship to board their ship. If they do not have it, they will not be allowed to board at the beginning of the cruise and will not receive a refund.

Open-Loop Cruises

If a cruise begins and ends in different U.S. ports, or begins and ends in a foreign port, a valid passport or other recognized document is required.

Recognized documents are defined by the Western Hemisphere Travel Initiative. Passports should be valid for at least six months beyond the end of the trip.

Travelers are advised to contact their cruise lines for updated information. For more information or changes to the regulations, go to the WHTI website.

Eastern Caribbean Cruise Ports in Brief

Eastern Caribbean cruise ports are close and convenient for many people living in the United States, which makes them a tempting choice for someone going on their first cruise.

Common departure ports are Miami and Fort Lauderdale in Florida for people who want the convenience of flying into Florida without any stopovers.

Typical eastern Caribbean cruise ports of call include:

Antigua

Antigua lays claim to having 365 beaches or one for every day of the year. Cruise visitors may not want to visit all 365, but instead head to a few of the best and most convenient.

Fort Bay beach, also known as Miller's Beach, is a 10-minute drive by taxi from the cruise port at St. John's. Other nearby beaches include Deep Bay, Runaway Bay and Dickenson Bay.

St. John's also has a nice shopping and dining district at the cruise docks. The island has an important historical attraction at English Harbour on the southeast end of the island.

Antigua also is a common stop on southern Caribbean cruises.

The Bahamas

No islands in the region has more visitors than the Bahamas because of numerous tourist attractions, recreational activities and shopping opportunities.

It is arguably the _most commercialized_ and will give visitors the most feeling of familiar settings. Nassau and Freeport are typical ports of call.

Treasure Cay Beach and Harbour Island Beach are two of the most popular and well-publicized beaches in the islands.

Duty free shopping includes _Port Lucaya Marketplace on Grand Bahama Island_ and Welcome Center at Festival Place on Nassau.

~~Port~~ Our Lucaya —

British Virgin Islands

BVI is a place of quiet beauty, beautiful beaches and great snorkeling and scuba diving.

Unique attractions include Dolphin Discovery, a chance to interact in the waters with dolphins; the historic forts Burt and Recovery, both dating back centuries; and Tortola's Main Street, which is both a shopping and historic district.

The most likely port of call is Tortola, the largest in this chain of dozens of islands.
They are closely packed together, which makes it easy for someone to make an excursion out of boating from one island to another.

Dominican Republic _Punta Canta ?_

DR is the _second most popular island overall_. Its main draw is its _plush_, numerous resorts on fantastic white sand beaches.

It is one of the few islands with whitewater rafting. Although people visit DR mostly to stay at the resorts, eastern cruises do stop there at cities such as La Romana.

San Juan, Puerto Rico

San Juan is a key stopping point and starting point for many cruises in the Caribbean. Old San Juan is one of the top tourist attractions in the region because of its history, architecture, shopping and quaint winding streets.

The shopping is extensive and the old Spanish forts are massive.

St. Kitts

The island of St. Kitts is a rising star in the Caribbean because of expansion projects that led to larger docks and more capacity.

St. Kitts has an attraction that is unique among Caribbean islands. The St. Kitts Scenic Railway is a narrow gauge train that takes visitors on a three-hour, 30-mile circular tour of the island.

An attraction that no one can miss is the 3,800-foot Mount Liamuiga, which dominates the center of this small island that is only 69 square miles. It is popular with hikers.

Brimstone Hill Fortress National Park, a UNESCO World Heritage Site built in 1690, is one of the best-preserved forts in the Caribbean.

Like Antigua, St. Kitts often appears on schedules for southern Caribbean cruises.

St. Lucia

The St. Lucia port city of Castries has one of the most beautiful harbors in the Caribbean.

The island has plenty of its own nice beaches, but nature lovers might want to visit its most famous landmark, the Pitons, which are a pair of dormant volcanoes more than 2,000 feet high. They also are home to an unusual attraction -- volcanic mud baths.

St. Lucia is another destination for visitors on both eastern and southern Caribbean cruises.

Turks and Caicos

Turks and Caicos is not two islands but 40 islands and cays. This British overseas territory -- like the nearby British Virgin Islands -- have become a popular stop for eastern Caribbean cruises. Cruise ships typically dock on Grand Turk.

Popular attractions include migrating humpback whales from January through April, the largest cave system in the Caribbean and a variety of historical tours.

U.S. Virgin Islands

The main cruise port at Charlotte Amalie, St. Thomas, is one of the most popular duty-free shopping meccas in the Caribbean.

It also offers excellent snorkeling. Cruise visitors can spend an easy afternoon at a good assortment of public beaches near the cruise port.

Western Caribbean Cruise Ports in Brief

Western Caribbean cruise ports deliver great excursions on Jamaica and Grand Cayman and great ecotourism in Belize and Costa Rica.

Many of the most famous Caribbean excursions and attractions are found in the western part of the region. All of them are outdoor, family oriented and require a moderate level of exertion.

Eight Western Caribbean cruise ports are popular:

- Cayman Islands
- Cozumel
- Jamaica
- Roatan
- Costa Rica
- Belize
- Panama
- Costa Maya

Each one has distinct reasons for being popular.

Cayman Islands

Stingray City is among the best and most memorable excursions. It also is among the most exciting and at the same time educational experiences. Visitors get onto a sandbar with three feet of water and interact with stingrays who have become comfortable with human contact.

Seven Mile Beach is one of the largest and best known beaches in the Caribbean. It is accessible right by the cruise port.

Another popular attraction is the Cayman Turtle Farm, which attracts 500,000 visitors a year, according to the farm's Web site. This breeding farm has 8,000 green sea turtles and has released more than 30,000 into the wild.

Cozumel

Beautiful beaches, Mayan ruins and a heavy emphasis on snorkeling and scuba diving are among the highlights of this popular Mexican island visit.

It also has a great shopping excursion across the water at Playa del Carmen's 5th Avenue, a long and pedestrian-only street lined with shops, hotels and restaurants. Cruise visitors who spend a day or more in Cozumel can take a ferry to Playa del Carmen.

Jamaica

The most famous waterfalls in the Caribbean are found at Dunn's River Falls, which visitors can climb to the top. It is one of the best excursions in the region and a memorable family experience. It is located near Ocho Rios, which also has the popular Dolphin Cove.

Ocho Rios and Montego Bay are the most active cruise ports in Jamaica, while Port Antonio and Falmouth are up and comers. Falmouth emphasizes Old Word history, culture and architecture.

Roatan

This up and coming island off the coast of Honduras is one of the less-developed destinations on a western cruise. It receives fewer visitors than most of the other destinations.

It is known for its beaches and especially for its snorkeling and scuba diving thanks to the second largest barrier reef in the world that stretches from this island down to Belize. For the same reason, Cozumel and Belize also are known for snorkeling and diving.

Costa Rica

Cruise visitors to Central American destinations usually embark from San Juan, New Orleans or Galveston because they are located farther south than the above islands.

While Cozumel emphasizes water recreation, Costa Rica focuses on the land. Many adventures are available in the rain forests involving hiking, canopying, gardens, rafting and more. The canopying high over the rain forests is a particular highlight.

Belize

This small nation may have the most well-balanced set of excursions. They include good snorkeling and diving, Mayan ruins, animal sanctuaries and more rainforest adventures.

But the overwhelming highlight is tubing on the Sibun River where tubers float through a series of underground caves that once were the location of Mayan rituals. Cave tubing on the Sibun is one of the best excursions in the Caribbean.

Panama

Multiple tours are available to see the Panama Canal in different ways. People can simply go to the locks to see how ships pass through. They also can kayak or boat in the canal itself or fish for freshwater bass in one of the lake's of the canal.

The tours aren't as exciting as others in the western Caribbean, but they are interesting and educational for children.

Costa Maya

Costa Maya is one of the smallest cruise ports in the western Caribbean, but like Roatan it is rising in popularity.

It lies about halfway between Cozumel to the north and Belize City to the south, which makes it a convenient stopover for cruises that go to both of those major destinations.

The port is mainly known for the nearby Mahahual beach, the town of

Mahahual about two miles away and the Mayan ruins at Kohunlich, Dzibanche and Kinichna. They are two hours away.

Cruise Weather / When to Go

Western Caribbean weather is known for heavy rainfall in the falls months, especially September and October. The heaviest rains falls in Belize and Costa Rica, which is why both countries have lush rain forests and popular ecotourism excursions.

The most popular time to take western cruises is December through April for people wanting to escape cold northern winters. Temperatures in the western Caribbean are warm this time of year, but it also is the time of year with the lowest risk of rain.

Waters are a bit cooler, so beach lovers may want to go in March or April. People who enjoy land activities and want to get away from the cold should visit from December through February.

Southern Caribbean Cruise Ports in Brief

Southern Caribbean cruise ports offer warm temperatures to northerners who want to escape cold winters.

The Caribbean Sea is more than 1 million square miles and 1,000 miles from the northern tip to the southern tip.

Temperatures in the south are often warmer than in the north. They matter to cruise visitors who want to spend time on beaches and in the seawater.

Daytime temperatures average in the mid 80s Fahrenheit during the winter and into the low 90s during the summer. Rainfall is low in the winter, spring and early summer. It jumps in the fall during hurricane season.

A large number of seven-day cruises to the southern Caribbean leave from San Juan, Puerto Rico, in order to reach the largest number of islands in the shortest period of time.

Southern Caribbean cruises often include ports that are listed on eastern and western cruises.

Ports of call often include:

Antigua

Unique attractions include Shirley Heights with its military fortifications and overlook of English Harbour and the historical Sea View Farm Village with displays of folk pottery.

The island also is known for having 365 beaches or one for every day of the year. One of the better ones that is close to the cruise docks is Miller's Beach. A taxi is the best way to get there; be sure to negotiate rate before getting into the cab.

Aruba

Aruba is one of the smaller southern Caribbean islands. It also is one of the most arid. It is known for Palm Beach, one of the best beaches in the Caribbean. It also is known for scuba diving among sunken ships.

Some southern Caribbean cruises also visit the nearby Curacao and the even smaller island of Bonaire.

Barbados

The island is one of the more commercial destinations in the Caribbean. But cruise visitors will find plenty of the usual island attractions plus a few that are unusual.

One of the best is swimming with sea turtles, a popular excursion just off the coast.

Unique attractions include the Flower Forest with a botanical garden and nature trail. Andromeda Natural Gardens has six acres of tropical plants and flowers. Harrison's Cave has underground streams and a 40-foot waterfall.

Dominica

Dominica is promoting itself as an ecotourism vacation and with good reason. It is one of the better hiking experiences in the Caribbean because of rain forests, mountains and waterfalls.

The cruise dock has a small tourist area that doesn't have the same level of shopping and dining as other destinations.

Anyone who likes hiking should consider a cruise with Dominica as a port of call. People who prefer beaches should consider a cruise that goes elsewhere.

San Juan

San Juan is a common departure port for southern Caribbean cruises. Tourists who fly into San Juan and have time to explore should consider going to Old San Juan, which is close to the cruise docks.

Old San Juan has two famous forts, cobblestone streets and a variety of historical and architectural attractions. It can easily fill anywhere from two hours to six hours of time before or after a cruise.

St. Kitts

St. Kitts had promoted itself as an ecotourism destination because it was quiet and undeveloped compared to some bigger islands.

It has taken a step up in recent years with a new cruise mall filled with shops, restaurants and entertainment. Visitors walk right off the docks and into the open-air mall.

The St. Kitts Scenic Railway is unique in the Caribbean. Guests can take a 30-mile route around the island and encircle the 3,800-foot Mount Liamuiga.

Other attractions include climbing a dormant volcano, many hikes, bird watching and the usual assortment of water sports.

St. Lucia

St. Lucia has a pretty cruise port and even prettier landscape in the interior of the island. We fondly remember an ATV excursion along the rugged coastline.

The most famous landmark is the Pitons, a pair of mountains that stand 2,000 feet over the island. Visitors there can hike, photograph and take volcanic mud baths. The views in the more remote part of the island are among the best in the Caribbean.

Other attractions include Pigeon Island National Landmark with a history of Amerindians, piracy and battles between the English and French. Fond d'Or Nature Historic Park has more island history, nature and culture. Fond Doux Estate is an authentic working plantation.

St. Maarten

This small but beautiful island has fewer attractions, although visitors are more likely to go because of cruises and for quiet overnight vacations.

Perhaps the best attraction on the island is the cruise port of Philipsburg. It is one of the best in the Caribbean because of its size and atmosphere.

Other attractions include the famous (and clothing optional) Orient Bay beach and the French towns of Marigot and Grand Case, which have the best restaurants on the island. I recommend the panoramic views atop Fort Louis and taking an excursion to the nearby St. Barts or Anguilla.

St. Thomas

St. Thomas isn't technically a southern Caribbean island, but southern Caribbean cruises often stop there on their way from San Juan.

Any list of attractions starts with shopping in the capital city of Charlotte Amalie on St. Thomas. Buck Island is one of the few fully protected marine parks in the United States.

Virgin Islands National Park includes an underwater reserve that makes up 5,650 acres. For these reasons, U.S. Virgin Islands abounds with snorkeling and diving opportunities.

Cruise Port Profiles

Antigua: St. John's

Eastern Caribbean

The Antigua cruise port at St. John's was hectic and filled with people on the day we arrived. It was no surprise because it is a popular stop for eastern Caribbean cruises.

Antigua attracts about 250,000 people a year for overnight vacations. But it attracts twice as many who stop for just the day on cruises.

One reason for the island's popularity with cruise visitors is the size and quality of the shopping district right by the docks at St. John's, the capital of Antigua.

Another possible reason is the fact that the island claims to have 365 beaches or one for every day of the year. That may be true, but many of them are small, so plan your beach visit.

We found the shopping to be good and the beaches to be average. But we enjoyed both anyway.

Quick Tips

- Antigua is known for shopping, beaches and historic attractions.
- Historical attractions at Nelson's Dockyard and English Harbour are especially well known.
- Taxis closest to the docks tend to charge the most.

Attractions and Shore Excursions

The cruise port of St. John's, capital of the islands, has one of the better shopping districts among major Caribbean cruise ports.

St. John's Cathedral, built in 1845, is a dominant attraction in the city with its white towers on a hilltop. The Museum of Antigua and Barbuda on Long Street, also in the city, is just a quarter mile northeast of the docks.

Grand Cayman has the famous Stingray City, where visitors get out of boats and hang out with friendly stingray on a sandbar. Antigua has its own version of it at Stingray Village. The "village" is a common shore excursion.

The historic Fort James and Fort James Beach are two and a half miles from the cruise docks. Passengers will need a taxi, rental car or excursion bus to reach them.

Other than St. John's itself, the best known attraction on the island is English Harbour. It is about 36 minutes by car from the cruise terminal on the southeast corner of the island.

English Harbour was considered the most important British Caribbean naval base from its beginning in the 1700s until its closure in 1889. The base is now part of the 15 square miles of Nelson's Dockyard National Park.

Points of interest there include Clarence House, a home built for the future King William IV (1765-1837) when he served under the legendary British admiral Horatio Nelson as captain of the H.M.S. Pegasus.

Like Grand Cayman, Antigua has a Stingray City where visitors can snorkel with stingrays in shallow water and even touch them. The attraction is a 30-minute drive on the eastern side of the island. It is available as a cruise line shore excursion.

Other attractions include Shirley Heights, a fortification overlooking English Harbour, and Half Moon Bay on the western tip of the island. It is a popular destination for walking, riding and the pink sand beach.

Nearby Beaches

Unlike some other Caribbean islands, Antigua does not have any good beaches right by the cruise terminal or within walking distance. So visitors will need a taxi, rental car or excursion bus to reach one.

Fort Bay Beach, which is about a 10-minute taxi ride from St. John's, also is known as Fort James Beach, because the ruins of Fort James lie at the southern tip. The fort doesn't have much left to see, but it has nice views of the St. John's harbor.

The beach is nice enough for an afternoon visit with white sand and a small number of nearby recreational activities, especially jet skis. Deep Bay also is located near St. John's.

Other major beaches with easy access from St. John's include the resort-dominated Runaway Bay and Dickenson Bay to the north of the city. Some cruise lines offer excursions to Long Bay Beach on the eastern side of the island.

To the south lie less-developed beaches that are somewhat more difficult to reach. They are Hermitage Bay, Galley Bay and Hawksbill Bay. Note that one of the four sections at Hawksbill is nudist.

The beach known as probably the best on the island is Half Moon Bay, but it is on the east side and farthest from St. John's. It is part of a national park and a good family choice because it is protected by a reef.

Shopping and Restaurants

Like most cruise ports, shopping is right there by the dock. The main shopping area is Heritage Quay; it is a three minute walk north of the cruise terminal. It has many stalls filled with colorful things to buy, some local and some not.

Redcliffe Quay is next to Heritage and provides more shopping and dining. Visitors who walk a little farther will find themselves on well-maintained streets with more traditional shopping.

Shopping near the docks tends to have less expensive and more authentic arts and crafts sold in stalls. Shops on the main streets had higher quality goods that were more commercialized and expensive.

Restaurants near the dock include:

- Big Banana 17°61°, Italian, at Redcliffe Quay
- Crazy Horse Saloon, bar and grill, lower Redcliffe Quay
- Chicken Hut, restaurant and bar, St. John's

Getting Around

Car rental agencies are mainly concentrated at V.C. Bird International Airport and in St. John's. But most agencies deliver cars to your location.

Check prices and availability for all of the agencies, call to see if the car will be delivered to your location and also call in advance to reserve a car.

Taxis are plentiful, and drivers will negotiate prices. When we negotiated a price to go from the cruise dock to Miller's Beach, our driver remained by the beach for more than two hours until we were ready to return. Public transportation in the form of buses was not available.

Weather / Best Times to Go

Antigua weather consists of warm temperatures year round that average in the mid 80s Fahrenheit.

The monthly high temperatures average about 83 degrees Fahrenheit in the winter and 87 degrees in the summer through mid-fall.

Rainfall is low from January through April, moderate in the late spring to mid-summer and reaches a high point from September through November during the annual Caribbean hurricane season.

Aruba: Oranjestad

Southern Caribbean

The Aruba cruise port of Oranjestad is a prime stop for southern Caribbean cruises. It is an easy island to tour in a short period of time, and the climate is almost always beautiful.

It doesn't hurt that Aruba also is one of the most popular destinations in the Caribbean because of its weather, beaches and things to do. It is one of our favorite destinations.

Cruise lines that visit Aruba including Holland, Princess, Carnival, Fred Olsen, PandO,Royal Caribbean, AIDA and Pullmantur.

Regardless of the cruise line, passengers will find many shore excursions to take on their own when they disembark at the port of Oranjestad, which is the capital of the island nation.

An iguana gets a suntan as an excursion boat passes in Aruba.

Quick Tips

- Taxis and buses provide quick, cheap and convenient transportation.
- Aruba is a beach destination. Definitely check out Palm Beach, only a 10-minute drive from the cruise terminal.
- The main shopping and dining are in Oranjestad (location of the cruise terminal) and Palm Beach.
- Likewise, nightlife is mainly found in the same two locations.
- The water sports are better than the land attractions.

Attractions and Shore Excursions

Palm Beach is the dominant attraction on the island. The beach is lined with hotels, resorts and restaurants that face Lloyd G. Smith Boulevard. The beach is great, and so is the nightlife.

The other side of the street in front of them is packed with shops and restaurants. Go to the Palm Beach Plaza at the north end of Smith Boulevard for free nightly entertainment.

Arikok National Park covers nearly one fifth of the island. It is a good option for touring a rough, arid and cactus-filled landscape via horseback, jeep or ATV. Cruise lines offer quite a few shore excursions to Arikok.

Arikok also has the remains of the famous natural bridge that collapsed in 2005, but it still has a few baby bridges. The view of the windy sea from the rock shores provides a peaceful respite. The nearby Natural Pool is another well-known attraction.

A bit farther north of Palm Beach is the California Lighthouse, one of Aruba's most famous landmarks.

The stone lighthouse was built in 1910 and named after a ship that sunk nearby. The site offers fantastic sunset views.

More adventurous souls with a taste for recreation should consider scuba diving because Aruba offers 42 major dive spots.

Nearby Beaches

Druif Beach and Surfside Beach are the closest to the cruise terminal. Both are walkable for energetic people who don't want to pay for a taxi, rental car or excursion bus.

Druif is about a 25 minute walk or nearly 1.5 miles to the north. Surfside is nearly the same distance to the south.

Otherwise, visitors should consider paying for transportation to the best beaches

Palm Beach is the best-known Aruba beach. It is famous and popular for its calm waters and location right next to a number of major resorts. The hotels and resorts have chairs, shade and watersports equipment for guests, while visitors may be able to buy refreshments.

Just south of Palm Beach is Eagle Beach, which has fewer hotels and people. It is wider than Palm and, like most beaches on Aruba, it has plenty of white sand. There are shaded picnic areas and parking spaces.

Other beaches including Arashi, Boca Catalina and Malmok have calm waters that make them ideal for swimming and snorkeling.

Be aware there are no nearby facilities, but the beaches are easily accessible by vehicle.

The beach at Hadikurari is known for windsurfing and is the site of the annual Aruba Hi-Winds Competition for both kiteboard and windsurfing. Picnic tables and shade huts are located there.

The widest beach on Aruba is at Punta Brabo, also known as Manchebo Beach. It is an extension of the nearby Eagle. The surf is stronger here, and no motorized water sports are permitted. Although accessible by vehicles, like Eagle it is quieter than Palm.

At the far southeast tip of the island are Baby Beach and Rodgers Beach. Baby Beach is a popular family location because of shallow and calm waters that are suitable for children. The nearby Rodgers is somewhat rougher and has limited facilities.

Shopping

The city is easily accessible from the cruise terminal and offers a large number of shopping opportunities on L.G. Smith Boulevard and some of the streets that run parallel to it.

Royal Plaza Mall, Renaissance Mall, and Seaport Village Mall and Marketplace all line L.G. Smith Boulevard within a few hundred yards of the cruise terminal.

The street also has a number of high quality open-air restaurants that are worth a visit for lunch or dinner.

Passengers with more time should take a taxi to Palm Beach, one of the best beaches in the Caribbean. It offers a good opportunity for shopping, dining, relaxing and swimming in one visit.

Restaurants

Restaurants are mainly concentrated in Oranjestad and Palm Beach. Oranjestad has a good supply of restaurants for the cruise visitor who wants to stay in town for a shorter period of time.

Many more restaurants are located on Palm Beach for anyone who wants to spend a longer day there eating, shopping and lounging on one of the best beaches in the Caribbean. Oranjestad restaurants include:

- Cuba's Cookin', Caribbean, Renaissance Marketplace on L.G. Smith Boulevard
- Driftwood, seafood, Klipstraat 12

- Iguana Joe's, American, 94 L.G. Smith Boulevard
- L.G. Smith's Chop and Steak House, chops and steaks, 82 L.G. Smith Boulevard
- Le Petit Cafe, seafood, 87 J.E. Irausquin
- The Paddock, international, 13 L.G. Smith Boulevard

Oranjestad restaurants include a mix of outdoor and indoor. Most of them are on L.G. Smith Boulevard, the main thoroughfare, and are within easy walking distance of the terminal.

Transportation / Getting Around

Getting around Aruba is quite easy. The island is small and public transportation readily available.

Reliable and cheap bus service is available between Oranjestad and resort areas. Taxis are always available and have set rates.

The island is small and easy to navigate, so renting a car is a good option for visitors who want to see it all. Most rental agencies are at the airport, but they have pickup and dropoff at the docks.

Driving is on the right side of the road. Foreign and international driving licenses accepted. Free parking is available throughout the island. Drivers cannot turn right at red lights.

Weather / Best Times to Go

If you are simply planning a Caribbean cruise that might include Aruba, it's good to know what to expect with weather.

Aruba weather is one of the warmest in the Caribbean. It maintains an average high temperature ranging from 86 degrees Fahrenheit in January to about 90 from May through November.

The island is quite arid with the lowest rainfall in the Caribbean. It averages only about one inch per month except for October through December, when it averages three inches.

During a February visit, we found the water chilly for swimming even though air temperatures were plenty warm. We were not alone in feeling that way. Few people spent time in the water.

Although Aruba lies below the Caribbean hurricane belt, it does feel the effects of nearby hurricanes and tropical storms during the peak bad weather season in the fall.

Bahamas: Nassau

Eastern Caribbean

Nassau is one of the most -- if not the most -- popular cruise ports in the Caribbean region.

Even though the Bahamas aren't in the Caribbean Sea properly, they serve as a common stop for many eastern Caribbean cruises. They also are the only destination for many cruises leaving from the East Coast of the United States.

Nassau on New Providence Island is the capital of the Bahamas. Major hotels and resorts are mostly concentrated at Cable Beach and the more expensive Paradise Island, a second small island of 685 acres that is connected to New Providence by two bridges.

Cruise visitors will arrive at the Prince George Wharf right by downtown Nassau. They can see Paradise Island and the massive Atlantis resort complex right from the docks.

The wharf can accommodate up to seven ships. Some days Nassau will be packed with visitors and other days it may be quiet.

Visitors will take a short walk on the docks, through the terminal and right into the downtown area. The terminal, known as Festival Place, has 45 artisans and shops along with tour information, a post office, communications center, phone cards, Internet access and information on taxis and ferry boats.

Once through the terminal, go one block south (in the opposite direction of the wharf) to reach Bay Street, the center of Nassau's tourism activity.

Quick Tips

- The Atlantis resort complex is the most popular attraction.
- Most beaches require transportation to reach them.
- The best time to visit for weather is late spring.

Attractions and Shore Excursions

Paradise Island is among the most popular attractions because of the Atlantis resort marine habitat, Dolphin Cay and the Predator Lagoon.

The island is accessible by bridge on the northeast coast of New Providence within a somewhat long walking distance from the cruise port. It is the well-developed complex of hotel and resort properties including Atlantis Paradise Island Resort & Casino. It has a water park, the world's largest open air marina, a massive hotel property and, of course, a large casino to go with it.

Other attractions include Blue Lagoon Island, which is 20 minutes away by sailboat and has beaches, snorkeling, diving and swimming with the dolphins.

Nassau is a popular golf destination throughout much of the year. Golf courses include Cable Beach Resorts Golf Club and South Ocean Golf & Beach Resort.

The Nassau Botanical Gardens and the nearby Ardastra Gardens, Zoo and Conservation Centre off Chippingham Road will appeal to nature lovers. They are right by Fort Charlotte and a somewhat lengthy one and a half miles from the cruise terminal.

Anyone with an interest in history will want to tour the local forts, especially Fort Charlotte, which is the largest on the islands, or forts Montagu or Fincastle. Charlotte is the best option among the forts.

The Queen's Staircase of Sixty Six Steps is right next to Fort Fincastle. The staircase is an impressive historical attraction that was hand carved out of solid rock. Fincastle and the Staircase are a half mile from Bay Street.

Nearby Beaches

The best beaches on New Providence and Paradise Island require a taxi, rental car or excursion bus to reach them. There is one beach within walking distance of the cruise terminal.

Junkanoo Beach, also known as the Western Esplanade, is a half mile west of the cruise docks. This area joins the beaches at Arawak Cay and Long Wharf. Go right as you walk out of the cruise terminal.

Cable Beach is more than two miles long and faces a series of top-rated hotels or resorts. It also has a golf course, nightlife and the largest casino in the Bahamas. It is six miles east of the terminal.

Three beaches lie parallel to Bay Street on New Providence island. They are Saunders and West Esplanade on the west side and Montague on the east side.

Paradise Island beaches include Colonial, Casuarina, Arawak and Smugglers. Cabbage Beach on Paradise Island has been called one of the best in the Caribbean.

Shopping / Restaurants

Nassau has a massive tourist district by the cruise docks and plenty of duty-free shopping. Popular shopping destinations include the straw markets, which showcase local arts and crafts, and Bay Street, which is lined with shops, cafes and restaurants.

Bay Street on New Providence is easily accessible from the cruise docks and runs parallel to the waterfront. Festival Place shopping is right by the docks, and the well-known Nassau Straw Market is nearby on Bay Street.

The Nassau Straw Market on West Bay Street is often packed with tourists because it is so close to the busy cruise docks.
FYI, the market doesn't sell plain straw. It sells a lot of souvenirs, arts and crafts. Only some of them are made out of straw.

Paradise Island has shops concentrated at Marina Village, Crystal Court (inside Atlantis Royal Towers) and The Craft Centre, which features local artisans.

Restaurants are heavily concentrated at Paradise Island, downtown Nassau and Cable Beach, which lies west of downtown and the cruise docks.

Getting Around / Transportation

Nassau is a rather odd port in that it calls for a lot of walking because of where everything is located.

Shopping is conveniently on Bay Street right by the cruise terminal. Other attractions range from a half mile to one and a half miles away. Moderately fit people may walk to most of them as we did, but it was a tiring day. Others might rely more on taxis and other transportation.

Taxi rates are set by the government according to zones on New Providence. Rates include the zones, the number of people, the number of baggages and wait time. There is no public bus system.

Several local and international rental car companies including Avis, Budget and Bowcar have locations in downtown Nassau that serve cruise visitors.

Weather / Best Times to Go

The best time to visit the Bahamas is in the spring, especially March, April or May. Cooler temperatures make the ocean water uncomfortable for swimming in January and February.

Nassau Bahamas has an average monthly high temperature of about 84 degrees Fahrenheit and the average monthly low is 69 degrees, according to the World Meteorological Organization.

The average high reaches its peak of 89 degrees from July through September and bottoms at less than 80 degrees from December through March. But the hottest months are some of the wettest.

Rainfall historically hits a high point in June and August, while July, September and October tend to have heavier rain as well.

At least seven inches or more falls each month from June through October. The wettest month of all is August, which has more than 9 inches of rain and 19 days of rain on average.

In contrast, December through March experience less than 2 inches of rain. Cool weather comes with the lower risk of rain.

Bahamas: Freeport

Eastern Caribbean

The cruise port at Freeport on Grand Bahama Island is the second most popular tourist destination in the Bahamas after Nassau.

Grand Bahama is one of the northernmost islands of the Bahamas. It is known for two areas in particular – the resort center at Freeport and the suburb of Lucaya. Cruise visitors will have a chance to see both of them.

Freeport is the dominant city on Grand Bahama with its own cruise terminal and the Grand Bahama Island International Airport. Lucaya also has a cruise terminal and is a major hub for cruise ships, shopping, restaurants, hotels and entertainment.

Quick Tips

- Port Lucaya Marketplace is a major tourist attraction.
- Grand Bahama has many beaches to offer, although none near the cruise port.
- March and April are two of the best months to visit for weather.

Attractions and Shore Excursions

Natural attractions include Lucayan National Park, which has one of the world's largest underwater cave systems. Peterson Cay National Park is a protected area a mile offshore with coral reefs and opportunities for picnicking, snorkeling and scuba diving.

Bahamas Dolphin Tours has swimming and diving with dolphins. It's a common excursion from the cruise lines. The facility is a short ferry ride from Lucaya.

Other favorite attractions are Rand Nature Center or the Garden of the Groves.

Rand Nature Center, 25 minutes from Freeport Harbor, is a common cruise line shore excursion. The 100-acre facility is a nature reserve with hiking trails and rotating visual art, cultural and educational exhibits.

Garden of the Groves, seven miles east of Port Lucaya Marketplace, is a botanical garden and family attraction with more than 10,000 species of plants and animals. It has 12 acres of waterfalls, gardens, a meditation labyrinth, petting zoo and playground.

Golfers can use two courses – the Grand Lucayan Reef Golf Course or Ruby Golf Course. Grand Lucayan near the Port Lucaya Marketplace has large and flat greens. Out of 18 holes, 13 play off water. The 18-hole Ruby Golf Course is closest to the Freeport Cruise Port at five miles or 12 minutes away. Both courses are par 72 and nearly 7,000 yards long.

Nearby Beaches

Grand Bahama has 90 miles of beaches on its southern shores that offer many options for anyone with transportation on their own. Otherwise, cruise lines offer plenty of excursion possibilities.

Xanadu Beach is the closest major beach to the Freeport Cruise Port at 15 minutes or six miles away. This public beach is three miles from the International Bazaar, offering water sports, straw goods, food and beverages.

The respectable Gold Rock Beach is a stretch for time at 30 miles or 40 minutes east of the cruise port.

Bahamas Ministry of Tourism recommends the smaller Paradise Cove Beach 13 miles or less than 30 minutes west of the port.

Finally, Taino Beach in Lucaya, has a children's playground, nature preserve and bird sanctuary.

Shopping / Restaurants

Shoppers will find plenty to browse and buy at the 12-acre Port Lucaya Marketplace. It is the place to go for any shoppers visiting Freeport by cruise and is a common cruise shore excursion.

Port Lucaya Marketplace is a nice shopping and restaurant district, although not nearly as big as the one in Nassau and other major ports. Still, visitors will find plenty to see and do both in the marketplace and at nearby attractions within walking distance such as Lucaya Beach and Windsor Park.

The older International Bazaar is closer to the Freeport cruise port but not as popular as Port Lucaya Marketplace. This mall is one of the oldest shopping areas in Freeport and is in decline.

Getting Around / Transportation

Taxi rates are metered and set by the government. Meter fares start at $3; each extra mile is 40 cent. Rates include another charge for every passenger over the age of two years old.

Grand Bahama has a bus system that runs from 7 a.m. to sunset. The fare is $1 in the Freeport and Lucaya areas and $2 in the west and east ends. Cruise visitors who disembark at the Freeport cruise port can take a bus or taxi to the Port Lucaya Marketplace.

Weather / Best Times to Go

Cruise visitors to Freeport will find plenty of warm weather throughout the year. Even during the winter, the average high temperature reaches the mid-70s Fahrenheit.

Average daytime temperatures eventually climb into the upper 80s Fahrenheit in the summer. But it's not the temperatures that may keep people away during some months of the year. It's the rainfall.

Rainfall averages two to three inches a month during the dry season from December through April. It rains less than 10 days a month during this time.

Rainfall begins to climb in May to four inches and eventually reaches the highest point of more than eight inches in August and September.

Cruise travelers planning to visit Grand Bahama will find that the best weather for a combination of warm temperatures and low risk of rain is in March and April.

Bahamas: All Ports in Brief

Eastern Caribbean

The Bahamas cruise ports are the most active in the Caribbean because they receive more than 3 million visitors a year -- the most in the entire region.

Eastern Caribbean cruises make the Bahamas a common stop because they are so close to Florida. The islands also attract cruises just to the Bahamas that last as briefly as three or four days.

The area is unique for the number of private islands owned by the cruise lines. Cruises often stop at these day-visit resorts.

Longer cruises include the various Bahamas cruise ports on their way to Turks and Caicos, the Virgin Islands and other popular stops on eastern cruises.

Nassau on New Providence island is the dominant port in the Bahamas. It is followed by Freeport on Grand Bahama island. Cruise lines also visit these private islands:

- Castaway Cay (Disney)
- Coco Cay (Royal Caribbean)
- Great Stirrup Cay (Norwegian Cruise Line)
- Half Moon Cay (Holland America Line and Carnival)
- Princess Cays (Princess Cruises, Regent Seven Seas)

Quick Tips

- Freeport and Nassau are the main cruise ports
- There are five major private cruise islands

- Best time to go is late spring to early fall

Following are brief profiles of the Bahamas cruise ports.

Nassau

Nassau on New Providence is the capital of the Bahamas. Cruise visitors will walk right off their ships, through the cruise terminal and into one of the largest shopping and dining districts for tourists in the entire Caribbean region. We could easily spend the entire afternoon there on our visits.

Major hotels and resorts are mostly concentrated at Cable Beach and the more expensive Paradise Island. It is a second small island of 685 acres that is connected to New Providence by two bridges.

Attractions. Besides the tourism district, attractions include Blue Lagoon Island, which is 20 minutes away by sailboat and has beaches, snorkeling, diving and swimming with the dolphins.

Nassau golf courses include Cable Beach Resorts Golf Club and South Ocean Golf and Beach Resort. The Nassau Botanical Gardens and Ardastra Gardens, Zoo and Conservation Centre will appeal to nature lovers.

Local historical attractions include Fort Charlotte, which is the largest on the islands, and the smaller forts Montagu or Fincastle. The Queen's Staircase of Sixty Six Steps, right by Fort Fincastle, is a popular tourist attraction that was hand carved out of solid rock. Fincastle and Queen's Staircase are a 15-minute walk from the tourism district.

Beaches. Cruise visitors will arrive at the Nassau port on the northeastern side of the island near Atlantis. If the cruise line offers any beach excursion, it is likely a visit to the five-mile long Atlantis beach.

The Atlantis towers are visible from the docks. Note the bridge to the east that crosses from New Providence Island to Paradise Island.

Junkanoo Beach, also known as the Western Esplanade, is within walking distance of the cruise docks. This area joins the beaches at Arawak Cay and Long Wharf. Take a right as you walk out of the cruise terminal.

The beaches here are popular with both tourists and locals. It has benches for sitting and viewing the ships that arrive or leave the harbor. Horseback and pony rides also are available.

Shopping and Restaurants. Nassau has plenty of duty-free shopping. Popular shopping destinations include the Straw Markets, which showcase local arts and crafts. They are a few blocks from the cruise terminals. Visitors just need to turn right outside of the terminal and walk only a few minutes to reach them.

Paradise Island has shops concentrated at Marina Village, Crystal Court (inside Atlantis Royal Towers) and The Craft Centre, which features local artisans.

Bay Street is the dominant shopping area and is lined with many shops, cafes and restaurants. It is easily accessible from the cruise docks and runs parallel to the waterfront. Festival Place shopping is right by the docks, and Straw Market is nearby on Bay Street.

Freeport

The Freeport cruise port is on Grand Bahama Island, which is the second most popular tourist destination in The Bahamas after Nassau and Paradise Island.

It is one of the northernmost islands of The Bahamas, the closest to Florida and is known for two areas in particular – the resort center at Freeport and the suburb of Lucaya.

Freeport is the dominant city on Grand Bahama with its own cruise terminal and the Grand Bahama Island International Airport. Lucaya also has a cruise terminal and is a major hub for cruise ships, shopping, restaurants, hotels and entertainment.

Attractions. Attractions include Lucayan National Park, which has one of the world's largest underwater cave systems, and Peterson Cay National Park, a protected area a mile offshore with coral reefs and picnicking, snorkeling and scuba diving.

Another favorite attraction is Pinder's Point Lighthouse, the birds and nature trails at Rand Nature Center or the Garden of the Groves, which has more than 10,000 species of plants and animals. Visitors can swim with the dolphins at Dolphin Experience Lagoon.

Shopping. Shoppers will find plenty to browse and buy at the 12-acre Port Lucaya Marketplace or at the International Bazaar, one of the oldest shopping areas in Freeport. It's a common shore excursion about a 20-minute drive from the cruise terminal.

We spent the afternoon there on a rainy day and found plenty to do, although it isn't as large as the Nassau district. It also has regular entertainment and can fill several hours of time during a shore excursion visit.

Golfers will be able to use two courses – The Lucayan Golf Course or The Reef Golf Course.

Castaway Cay

Castaway Cay is Disney's private port and provides activities such as snorkeling, boating, swimming and sunbathing. Amenities include:

- Private and furnished cabanas at Castaway Family Beach (for families) and Serenity Bay Beach (for adults)
- Two water play areas
- The Hide Out, a teens-only activity area on the beach
- Open-air BBQ dining locations, two shops with gifts and souvenirs, and tram transportation
- Swimming, kayaking, water sports and other activities at the various areas
- Open-air massages with an ocean view, a yoga class and a bar at the secluded, adults-only beach, Serenity Bay
- Excursions including stingray interactions, glass-bottom boat tours, parasailing and fishing
- Free childcare at Scuttle's Cove, a child's area supervised by Disney counselors
- Disney Character Greetings, including a Dance Party with Lilo and Stitch

Coco Cay

Coco Cay, just south of Freeport, is a private island owned by Royal Caribbean. Amenities include:

- Hiking, parasailing and kayaking
- Waverunners, the most popular activity
- Caylana's Aqua Park, a floating playground
- Seaside barbecues
- Snorkeling among sunken wrecks

This private island doesn't have any restaurants or shops, but the private beach offers mixed and frozen drinks.

Great Stirrup Cay  *Oceania*

Norwegian Cruise Line owns Great Stirrup Cay, which is north of Nassau. Amenities include:

- WaveRunners and parasailing
- Snorkeling
- Kayaking and boat tours
- Complimentary dining.
- Straw market; Bahamas arts and crafts for purchase.
- Kids play area and Hippo water slide

Half Moon Cay

Half Moon Cay is farthest south and east of any Bahamas cruise port. Holland America Line and Carnival Cruise Lines use it more than other cruise lines. Amenities include:

- Horseback riding
- Snorkeling
- Stingray interaction in Stingray Cove.
- Shore excursions
- Two-mile beach
- Children's water park
- Interior lagoon

Princess Cays

Princess Cays is a 40-acre resort owned by Princess Cruises on the island of Eleuthera. The island is 100 miles long and only two miles wide. Amenities include:

- A half-mile beach
- Observation tower
- Complimentary beach barbecue
- Local craft market
- Beach volleyball
- Water sports equipment

Barbados: Bridgetown

Eastern Caribbean

A Barbados cruise port visitor may be disappointed to walk out on the deck on arrival at the cruise terminal and get a first glimpse of this popular Caribbean island. It all looks so ... commercial.

Barbados is a fairly large island for a southern Caribbean cruise port -- 166 square miles -- and a fairly populated one at 300,000 people.

It also gets populated with tourists. A half million people visit the island every year for overnight vacations, the Caribbean Tourism Organization says. Another half million visit by cruise.

The cruise port at Bridgetown is used heavily for commercial freight and other needs of this bustling former British colony.

A Barbados cruise port visitor may be disappointed to walk out on the deck on arrival at the cruise terminal and get a first glimpse of this popular Caribbean island. It all looks so ... commercial.

Barbados is a fairly large island for a southern Caribbean cruise port -- 166 square miles -- and a fairly populated one at 300,000 people.

Constitution River divides the city of Bridgetown. The view is from the bridge by Independence Arch.

It also gets populated with tourists. A half million people visit the island every year for overnight vacations, the Caribbean Tourism Organization says. Another half million visit by cruise.

The cruise port at Bridgetown is used heavily for commercial freight and other needs of this bustling former British colony.

But cruise visitors need not worry. They will find Barbados has plenty of things to do, food to eat and tropical beaches for sunning.

Quick Tips

- The Barbados cruise terminal is located right at Bridgetown. No need for transportation to shop or dine, although getting to the best of Barbados is a mile walk.
- The main thoroughfare is Broad Street, which has most of the duty-free shopping and historic attractions.
- Snorkeling with sea turtles is one of the best unique excursions.
- Beaches are accessible by taxi, bus or car rental.

Attractions and Shore Excursions

Moderately fit cruise visitors who don't want to pay for a taxi will need to walk a mile or more to get to some of the better attractions, shopping and dining in the city. For us, we didn't mind on our first visit. On the second visit, the heat encouraged us to take a taxi.

Broad Street is the place to go. It has some of the city's historic attractions, such as St. Mary's Anglican Church, built in 1825, and the Barbados Parliament Building, which has a beautiful clock tower and vaulted windows.

St. Michael's Cathedral, which was built in the mid-17th century, is nearby as well. We also enjoyed lunch on a warm and breezy day overlooking Constitution River right by the Independence Arch.

Outside of the city, one of the best experiences on the island is snorkeling with sea turtles.

Visitors will take a boat out of Bridgetown to a nearby location, just off the coast, where a large number of hawksbill sea turtles gather that have become comfortable with human contact.

Visitors can snorkel with the turtles while guides feed them. The turtles come within just a few feet of people in the water, but they veer away if anyone comes too close.

Harrison's Cave, a stream system more than a mile long, is a popular attraction. It also is a common shore excursion of the cruise lines. The cave is 10 miles northeast of the cruise terminal and requires a taxi, rental car or excursion bus to reach it.

Other attractions include the Flower Forest, which has 50 acres of flowers, animals and trails; Andromeda Natural Gardens with six acres of flora and fauna; and Ocean Park, a marine aquarium with 26 exhibits.

The island has seven golf courses at last count. Sandy Lane, Rockley and the Rockley Tree Plum courses are closest to the Bridgetown cruise port.

Nearby Beaches

Beach lovers will find more than 60 of them stretched across 70 miles of sand. The best of the bunch is Crane Beach in St. Philip parish, according to Barbados Tourism Marketing. It is located on the other side of the island and is a 40-minute drive from Bridgetown.

Visitors simply wanting to spend time on the beach should note that the Barbados cruise port is located on the southwest coast of the island.

Anyone who doesn't want to take the time to go to Crane Beach will find three popular beaches just north of the capital.

One of the most popular beaches for cruise visitors is Brandons Beach, which is 1.5 miles north of Bridgetown. It offers water sports, restaurants and plenty of activity.

Brighton Beach lies just next to Brandons. Batts Rock, another beach near Bridgetown has picnic areas, playground, facilities and shade trees.

Another group of beaches lies to the south starting at 1.5 miles from the cruise terminal. They are Brownes, Bayshore and Pebbles, although they really make up just one beach. They are available as a cruise line shore excursion.

Shopping / Restaurants

Shopping is the first option for any visitor because passengers will walk right off the ship and into the Bridgetown Cruise Terminal in the bustling capital of Barbados.

The terminal has more than 60,000 square feet of space with 20,000 square feet dedicating to shopping. Most of the shops are duty free and offer typical tourist items.

Outside of the main entrance, Chattel Village has 16 more shops in a courtyard environment.

From there, visitors will need to walk or drive about a mile to get to the city center of Bridgetown.

Broad Street provides the bulk of the duty-free shopping. Cave Shepherd is a shopping center on Broad Street and provides some of the best variety in duty-free shopping.

Those looking for local crafts should travel a little farther down the road to Pelican Village, where a wide selection of handcrafts, art and local food is available. Walkers will find it about halfway between the cruise terminal and city center.

Broad Street lies along Constitution River with some restaurants offering nice views along the opposite bank.

Broad Street offers higher-end shops with duty-free shopping. The more interesting experience lies along Swan Street, which runs parallel to Broad. This cobblestone, pedestrian-only street is popular with local and has many shops and street vendors.

Transportation / Getting Around

The government transit board and private operators provide taxis and minibuses. Taxis are not metered, so confirm the price before getting into the cab.

Government buses are blue with a yellow stripe. There are two terminals in Bridgetown and one in Speightstown.

Car rental agencies are common on this island that is 21 miles long and 14 miles wide in part because beaches, resorts and other major attractions are widely dispersed. Many of the agencies serve the cruise terminal.

Visitors must drive on the left side of the road as common with British and former British territories.

Weather / Best Times to Go

Barbados weather maintains an average high temperature of about 83 degrees Fahrenheit from December through March.

The average high starts to climb in April and hovers around 87 degrees from June through October.

Rainfall is light in the winter and spring, moderate in the summer and heavy in the fall.

Total rainfall is about two inches a month from January through April and peaks at more than five inches in September through November.

Late spring is the best time to visit Barbados for a combination of warm temperatures and low risk of rain.

The most popular months to visit are January, March and especially December.

Belize: Belize City

Western Caribbean

Belize City is a popular western Caribbean cruise port, but the surrounding countryside has much more to offer.

Passengers will arrive at the cruise terminal and the Belize City Cruise Village, which offers the most convenient shopping and dining.

The rest of the city offers cultural centers, historical centers and colonial architecture along with the usual shopping, bars, nightlife and restaurants. Cultural and historical attractions in the city include the House of Culture, Museum of Belize and St. John's Cathedral.

But even more appealing is the wealth of archaeological and eco-related attractions found nearby in other parts of the country.

One of the best things about the country of Belize is that its small size makes it easy to visit many of nation's attractions. They include sites that can be done as day trips from Belize City.

Attractions and Shore Excursions

Mayan Ruins of Altun Ha

Ruins of the Mayan civilization are found throughout Belize with one major site only 30 miles north of Belize City. Known as "Altun Ha", these are the closest and most accessible Mayan temple-pyramids to Belize City.

Nevertheless, most folks visit Altun Ha on a day tour because reaching the site with public transportation involves a two mile hike through hot and humid jungle.

Quick tours to Altun Ha are done by bus. Folks who want to make a day of it should go for one of the tours that begins with a three-hour boat ride up the Belize River. It is followed by lunch on the riverbank and a bus ride to the ruins.

Those who fantasize about being Indiana Jones can also hire a local guide to lead them on a long, hot walk to the site via jungle trails.

Belize River Boat Tours

The Belize River runs through Belize City and acts a conduit to the country's north-central interior.

During colonial times, British lumber operations used this waterway to transport valuable mahogany from the rainforests of the interior.

Some centuries before the British showed up, the Mayans used the Belize River to link their cities with the Caribbean Sea.

At present times, it's mostly used for more light-hearted purposes such as transportation to and from eco-lodges and for boat tours in search of Belize wildlife.

A boat tour on the river makes for an excellent, exciting break from the hustle and bustle of Belize City. Tours are typically half day excursions although guides don't complain when visitors to Belize City opt for a full day of adventure on the river.

Some of the more frequently encountered animals are stately herons, egrets, and storks, prehistoric looking crocodiles, iguanas, and Black Howler Monkeys that sit in the branches of riverside trees.

Cave Tubing and Jungle Exploration

Adventurous visitors to Belize City won't want to miss a tour that begins with a hike or an ATV ride along jungle trails in the Sibun Caves Branch Archaeological Park.

It includes a bit of Mayan cave exploration and a short guided walk through the Belizean rainforest.

At the end of the trip, visitors will jump into an inner tube and float through an underground river that had been the site of Mayan religious rituals.

They wear headlamps to see their way down the slow-moving river as a guide explains the both the Mayan past and the cave's natural history.

It's a lot for one day, but hundreds of visitors to Belize City opt for this exciting tour. We did as a family, and it remains one of our favorite shore excursions in the Caribbean.

Note that the Belize Zoo lies along the same route and takes about 45 minutes to reach from Belize City cruise port. Cave tubing is a five- to six-hour trip and usually costs $75 to $100 per person with discounts for young children.

Community Baboon Sanctuary

Black Howler Monkeys in Belize (where they are known as "baboons") have become endangered due to deforestation in their already small range.

Fortunately, there are conservation efforts to ensure the future of these unique primates, the most important of which is the Community Baboon Sanctuary.

A day trip to the visitor center for this site is an excellent way to learn about and see these rare monkeys up close and personal and is also a good way to meet the friendly folks of rural Belize.

The sanctuary is located about 50 minutes west of the Belize City cruise port.

The Blue Hole

This attraction appeals almost entirely to scuba divers. The Blue Hole is a collapsed cave off the coast of the country that is 407 feet deep and 1,050 feet wide, according to the Belize Tourism Board.

The site, which is part of the Lighthouse Reef Atoll, is known as one of the best dive sites in the world because of its depth, hammerhead sharks and stalactite formations.

It is about 43 miles east of the cruise port.

Nearby Beaches

Belize is not a beach destination because most of the shoreline consists of mangrove forests. Cruise lines offer few to no excursions that go to any beaches because the few that exist are mostly small or too far away.

There is one small man made beach about two miles west of the cruise terminal at Old Belize.

Otherwise, cruise visitors should plan on visiting beaches at other Caribbean ports. Belize is the place for rainforests, Mayan temples and cave tubing.

Shopping / Restaurants

Belize City is not known for its tourist shopping and restaurant district like other Caribbean destinations. It is better known as the starting point for excursions into the interior.

It does have two well-known shopping centers at the Fort Street Tourism Village and the nearby Belizean Handicraft Market Place, 2 South Park Street. Fort Street has about 30 gift shops; the Market Place emphasizes local arts and crafts.

Note that cruise lines offer very few city or shopping tours for Belize City.

Weather / Best Times to Go

Belize City has a brief dry season from February through April when the average rainfall is about two inches per month.

Average high temperatures are in the low 80s Fahrenheit in February and increase to the upper 80s by April. It's the best time to visit by cruise.

The rainy season hits hard starting in June and continues through December. The average rainfall increases to more than 10 inches a month during the fall. Average high temperatures stay in the upper 80s

Fahrenheit. January is a transition month between the dry and rainy seasons with an average rainfall of about five to six inches.

Bermuda: Hamilton and King's Wharf

Eastern Caribbean

Bermuda in the Atlantic Ocean, which lies about 600 miles east of North Carolina, attracts two kinds of cruise visitors: People who who cruise there as their only stop and people on ships that stop there on their way to the eastern Caribbean.

This small British territory consists of small islands connected by bridges and causeways. From end to end, the country measures only 22 miles long. Tourists can travel the entire length in about one hour.

Visitors will enjoy bright blue skies, pink sand beaches, golf courses, museums and historic sites. It also has plenty of high-end boutiques and dining options.

Bermuda is not a vacation for anyone on a budget. Plan to spend some cash when going ashore. Dining and shops are pretty pricey.

These islands are more conservative than the others in the Caribbean. Restaurants have dress codes, and visitors can stroll around in bathing suits only on the beaches.

Parents will be happy to know that Bermuda is a great destination for families with many kid-friendly activities. There are many city attractions, and the beaches are clean and safe.

No need to worry about a language barrier either, English is spoken everywhere here.

Quick Tips

- Cruise ships usually dock at King's Wharf or Hamilton.
- Royal Navy Dockyard is the most popular attraction.
- Excursion buses may offer a more budget friendly option for touring the island than taxis.

Destinations / Ports of Call

Ports of call for Bermuda cruises will depend on the itinerary chosen. The most common itinerary is a five- to seven-night package with the only stop being Bermuda.

Ships will dock at King's Wharf on the northwest tip of the island for two to three nights. Some may also stop at Hamilton in the island's center or St. George's at the northeast tip.

King's Wharf

This wharf is where all the major cruise lines dock. Ships will stop right inside the Royal Naval Dockyard (the most popular tourist site of the islands).

King's Wharf is rich with history and home to the Bermuda Maritime Museum. There is a mall, lighthouse and art center in the vicinity.

Buses, taxis and scooters can takes guests away from the busy area if they prefer some more private spots for relaxation.

Hamilton

The capital of Bermuda is Hamilton with plenty to see and do. Cruise ships usually dock right at Front Street where all the action takes place.

Hamilton has many daytime and nighttime activities, and visitors can see the entire town on foot. Public transportation is available for those that don't want to walk.

St. George's

St. George's was the first colonized location on Bermuda and is now a World Heritage Site. This charming island is full of history and beautiful architecture.

Visitors can stroll along cobblestone streets and enjoy the scenery.

Attractions and Shore Excursions

Bermuda Maritime Museum is at the Royal Naval Dockyard. It was officially opened by Queen Elizabeth II in 1975.

It houses some of Bermuda's most extensive artifact collections including rare treasures from the 16th and 17th centuries.

Another attraction within walking distance of the docks is Dolphin Quest, a dolphin interactive experience.

Commissioner's House built in 1820 was once home to the Dockyard Commissioner. It is a large Georgian House and the first ever cast iron house in the world. Guests can explore the house and see collections and exhibits of that time period.

At Bermuda Craft Market, guests can stroll through 60+ local art stands in the old cooperage building in the dockyard. It's a five-minute walk north of King's Wharf next to Dolphin Quest.

View or buy artwork and handicrafts including paintings, jewelry, woodwork and candles.

Nearby Beaches

Snorkel Park is a white sand beach at the west end of Bermuda. It is within the dockyard complex, and cruisers can walk there from ships that dock at King's Wharf.

The water is calm and perfect for children to enjoy the ocean. Snorkelers will spy colorful fish and coral reefs under the turquoise waters.

Black Bay Beach is ideal for swimming and snorkeling in its shallow waters. The waves are calm, but swimmers should be aware of sharp rocks.

The sand is soft and covered with sea glass. There is a concession stand in the area to rent umbrellas, chairs and other beach items.

Shopping / Restaurants

Along with the Bermuda Craft Market by King's Wharf, there are quite a few other options for die-hard shoppers. Although there is no sales tax in Bermuda, items are not cheap due to import duties.

There are shopping centers in Hamilton City (along Front Street), at Somers Wharf in St. George's and at the Clocktower Mall by the Royal Naval Dockyard.

Some of the more unique finds in Bermuda are Gombey Rag Dolls, Banana Leaf Dolls, Longtail Jewelry and Rum Cakes.

The Pickled Onion serves authentic Bermudian food along with Asian and

Latin menu items. The restaurant offers views of Hamilton Harbor.

Black Horse Tavern has Bermudian and Continental food with a casual atmosphere. It is a place where locals like to dine with reasonable prices.

Somerset Country Squire Pub and Restaurant is a traditional British Pub with average prices and a terrace overlooking Mangrove Bay.

Polaris at Carriage House has water views and Bermudian cuisine including seafood and sushi. Local fish and lobster caught fresh are on the daily menu.

Getting Around

Passengers who disembark from ships at King's Wharf will need transportation to get to Hamilton, which is 15 miles away.

Shore excursion buses are common and often include visits to both Hamilton and St. George's. These excursions may cost $100 per person or more. Otherwise, taxis have metered rates set by the government. Exact change is required.

The rate for a one- to four-passenger taxi is $7.90 US for the first mile and $2.75 US for each extra mile. The rate for a five- to seven-passenger taxi is $9.95 US for the first mile and $3.50 US for each extra mile.

The expense of getting from King's Wharf to Hamilton by taxi and back may make an excursion bus a better option.

The island has a convenient public bus system with 11 routes and 14 zones. Most buses leave from the Central Terminal on Washington Street by City Hall in Hamilton.

Bermuda also has a ferry system. Ferries leave from the Ferry Terminal on Front Street in Hamilton.

Weather / Best Times to Go

Bermuda has sub-tropical weather with high humidity and warm temperatures. Average high temperatures from December through March hover in the 60s Fahrenheit.

April through November are warmer months with average highs in the 70s and 80s Fahrenheit.

Bermuda does not have a monsoon or rainy season. There is no fixed pattern for rainfall, but October is generally the wettest month with an average of six inches of rain. April is the driest month with three inches of rain.

The best time to visit Bermuda is from April to September. The temperatures are warmer, along with the water.

The majority of tourist attractions are open during this time. Those who prefer to go when there are fewer people should visit during the winter months. The winter is popular with golfers.

Bonaire: Kralendijk

Western Caribbean

The tiny Dutch island of Bonaire is a port of call now and then with Panama Canal and southern Caribbean cruises. Ships that visit it usually stop at the nearby Aruba or Curaçao as well.

Among the three, known as the ABC islands, Bonaire is the least commercialized because it receives fewer visits. The lack of commercialization may appeal Caribbean visitors who get tired of it on other islands.

Cruise visitors will find that it has a few qualities in common with Aruba: nice beaches, plenty of snorkeling and diving, and an arid landscape.

Quick Tips

- Bonaire is famous for diving and snorkeling.
- Four beaches are near the cruise port.
- The island has taxis and rentals cars but no public transportation.

Attractions and Shore Excursions

Bonaire attractions emphasize diving and snorkeling. The waters off the coast of the island have been legally protected as a marine park since 1979.
Cruise visitors who don't snorkel or dive will find other things to do.

Willemstoren Lighthouse is a photographic pink, white, red and yellow lighthouse and an historical landmark built in 1837. It is on the most southern point of the island 10 miles south of the cruise port at Kralendijk.

The arid Washington/Slagbaai National Park has hiking trails among the spare landscapes of cacti, iguanas and divi-divi trees as well as dry forest, mangroves, beaches and sand dunes.

The park was the first nature sanctuary of the Netherland Antilles islands when it was created in 1969.

Wildlife includes parrots, flamingos, parakeets, iguanas and all four species of Caribbean nesting turtles. The visitors' center has a museum and walking trails.

The Donkey Sanctuary four miles south of Kralendijk is a non-profit foundation that provides care for the donkeys on Bonaire. The animals greet visitors when they arrive at the park, which is open 10 a.m. to 5 p.m. daily.

Fort Oranje, which was built in 1639, never saw action. The cannons are old English cannons that date between 1808 and 1812. It now serves as a courthouse.

The Butterfly Garden is open from Tuesday till Sunday. Opening hours are from 9 am till 5 pm. Take the road from the church in Kralendijk to Sorobon (Kaya Nikiboko Zuid). After leaving Kralendijk you will see the sign on the left. Turn to the left in the direction of Lac Cai and you will see the signs to the garden.

Bonaire National Marine Park is known as one of the better snorkeling experiences in the Caribbean. A narrow fringing reef starts near the shoreline and extends nearly 1,000 feet offshore.

The 1000 Steps snorkel and dive site on the north side of Bonaire is reachable by boat or car. Anyone who drives there actually will take 67 steps to reach the beach.

The island has 86 official dive sites and 53 easily accessible shore dive sites. Most of the sites are marked with yellow stones and are found on the roadside. Each stone has the name of the site.

Anyone who uses Bonaire waters is required to buy a nature tag. It is $25 for divers and $10 for all other users.

One of the unique attractions and an excursion offering by some tour operators on the island is related to salt. Salt pans are flat expanses of ground covered with salt that has evaporated from seawater. Bacteria changes the salt into various colors.

Bonaire is one of the world's major exporters of salt because of the salt pans, which also have become something of a tourist attraction on the island. The salt pans also are an ideal site to view flamingos.

Nearby Beaches

Bonaire makes it easy for cruise visitors to find a beach with 22 of them scattered around this small island and four right by the Kralendijk cruise port.

Most of the beaches are on the western side of the island where Kralendijk is located as well.

Almost all Bonaire beaches are public except for Sorobon, a clothing-optional beach in a private nudist resort where non-guests pay $10 for admission.

Four beaches close to Kralendijk are Bachelor's, Te Amo and Flamingo, along with one of the most unusually named beaches in the Caribbean. It is called Chachacha.

Some cruise shore excursions take visitors to Coco Beach, two miles north of the cruise terminal and next to a resort.

Bachelor's Beach is a small beach just south of the docks. It lies below a 10-foot cliff, according to Tourism Corporation Bonaire.

Te Amo is a white-sand beach near Bonaire's airport. Visitors can watch planes leaving and landing close up on the beach.

Flamingo at Divi Flamingo Beach Resort is a 10-minute walk from the center of Kralendijk.

Chachacha, named after a local woman, is a small beach with a wooden pier. The waters are calm and ideal for families with young children.

Pink Beach, the longest beach on the island, has fine pink sand. It is a popular spot for sunbathing and swimming. It is seven miles south of the port.

The beach has been featured on the cover of Caribbean Travel. Life magazine named it one of the best beaches in the Caribbean. A bus goes there throughout the day.

Visitors to Washington-Slagbaai National Park will find three major beaches at Boca Cocolishi, Boca Slagbaai and Playa Funchi.

Boca Cocolishi on the north coast is not well-suited for swimming because of the strong surf. But it is a black sand beach with lava-formed pools that make it appealing for hikers.

Boca Slagbaai, popular with the flamingos, is a good swimming and snorkeling site. It has facilities and refreshments for sale. Some of the buildings there date back to 1869.

Playa Funchi is a highly recommended snorkeling site because of coral formations, attractive fish and calm waters. It has no sand or facilities, although it is likewise popular with flamingos.

Shopping / Restaurants

Kayi Grande is Bonaire's main shopping street for tourists and runs parallel to the cruise docks.

The Bonaire Arts and Crafts Cruise Market is by the north and south piers in downtown Kralendijk. Anyone who arrives at the north pier can walk directly into the market in Wilhelmina Plaza. Passengers who arrive at the south pier can turn left at the road and walk a short distance to reach the market.

Harbourside Mall, 31 Kaya Grande, has a variety of shops and restaurants.

Many shops close for lunchtime. They are open Monday through Saturday from 9 a.m. to noon and again from 2 p.m. to 6 p.m. Some shops stay open through lunch hours, Sundays and Holidays.

Getting Around / Transportation

The island has a population of less than 20,000 people, so it's no surprise that public transportation is minimal. The island does not have a bus system.

Taxis, rental cars and excursion buses are the main means of getting around the island.

More adventurous visitors can rent bicycles and motor scooters to get around the island, which is barely 10 miles across.

Weather / Best Times to Go

Bonaire climate shares similar characteristics with nearby Aruba and Curaçao.

Temperatures are steady all the year and vary only a few degrees each month. It has much less rainfall than the rest of the Caribbean and only a slight increase in rain during the fall months.

Thanks in part to its southern Caribbean location, the average high temperature throughout the year is 87 degrees Fahrenheit or 31 degrees Celsius. The average low temperature, which takes place mostly at night, is 78 degrees Fahrenheit or 26 degrees Celsius.

Rainfall averages one inch a month from January through September. The worst months are October, December and especially November, when it averages 4 inches. It has only slightly more rain than the nearby Aruba.

British Virgin Islands: Road Town

Eastern Caribbean

The British Virgin Islands, located in the heart of the Caribbean, are an equally popular destination for cruise lines and overnight visitors.

The islands, which are made up of more than 50 islands, attract nearly 400,000 cruise visitors and about as many who stay at hotels and resorts.

About 15 of these islands are inhabited. Tortola, Virgin Gorda, Anegada, and Jost Van Dyke are the largest islands in the group.
The capital of the British Virgin Islands is Road Town, located on the island of Tortola. It also is the main cruise port.

Being the largest island on the chain, Tortola has the most to do in terms of attractions, accommodations and restaurants.

Attractions and Shore Excursions

The British Virgin Islands may be unique in that one of the best attractions is simply ferrying around the many islands in the chain, even in one day.

Ferrying will take cruise visitors to the islands' famous natural attractions, such as the Baths at Virgin Gorda.

Most of Road Town can be explored on foot. Shopping and restaurants are located within walking distance of the port.

Although touring Tortola itself is a popular activity for cruise visitors, the country's 21 national parks are a big draw for anyone who likes beaches, hiking, tropical forests, bird sanctuaries and shipwrecks.

Historic sites in Road Town include Britannic Hall, Her Majesty's Prison, Old Government House, Sir Olva Georges Plaza and Virgin Islands Folk Museum.

Forts Burt and Recovery are near Road Town. Burt was originally built on a hill overlooking the harbor to defend the town. The foundations and magazine remain of this historic ruin rebuilt in 1776. The site is free and open daily. It is a two-mile walk or drive southwest of town.

Fort Recovery was built in the 1640s as a military gun post. The ruins are intact and are the oldest historical landmark in Tortola. It is a five-mile drive southwest of Road Town.

The parks located on Tortola include J.R. O'Neal Botanic Gardens, Mount Healthy, Sage Mountain and Shark Bay.

J.R. O'Neil is a 3-acre park in the middle of Road Town. Mount Healthy features the remains of a thickly walled stone windmill that used to be part of an 18th century sugar plantation. Sage Mountain is the highest point in the U.S. and British Virgin Islands at 1,719 feet and offers expansive views of the area. Shark Bay is a nature preserve and the territory's first coastal park.

One of the most popular excursions in Tortola is the Discovery Dolphin Swim. This interactive dolphin program gives children and adults alike the opportunity to kiss, hug, and swim with a dolphin.

The Discovery Dolphin excursion costs $84 for adults and $73 per child.

A private tour of Tortola and deep sea port fishing make for other great excursion opportunities.

Nearby Beaches

The most popular beach and one often called one of the best beaches in the Caribbean is Cane Garden Bay. It is a 25-minute drive from Road Town on the east side of Tortola near Callwood Rum Distillery.

This sheltered and curved bay is popular with boaters because it lacks heavy winds. It also attracts swimmers, windsurfers and local residents. Because of its popularity, it also has a number of bars and restaurants.

Nearby and to the northeast of Cane Garden Bay is Brewer's Bay Beach. It is known for the ruins of old plantations and distilleries and for the snorkeling among the reefs.

Some cruise lines and excursion operators offer a 30-minute trip to Long Bay Beach at Beef Island.

Shopping / Restaurants

The Road Town cruise terminal has a complex of shops and restaurants. But Main Street is the place to go for the biggest concentration of shopping and dining.

A few of the restaurants in the town include C&F Bar and Restaurant, Calypso Cafe, Charlie's Restaurant, Drakes Point, Le Grand Cafe, Marche, Maria's by the Sea, Mariner Inn, Midtown, Nature's Way, Origin Kitchen and Bar, Pusser's Pub and Grill, Roti's Palace, Sharky's Mexitalian Grill, Simply Delicious, The Pub, The Watering Hole, Verandah, and Virgin Queen Restaurant & Pub.

Jost Van Dyke and Virgin Gorda

Jost Van Dyke is easy to reach from Tortola by ferry. The island is home to beautiful beaches and some of the most popular and unique bars in the British Virgin Islands.

The Soggy Dollar, a famous swim up bar and legendary creator of the Painkiller, is located on White Bay.

Virgin Gorda is the second largest of the British Virgin Islands and popular for cruisers because it is far less crowded than Tortola. From Tortola, cruise lines often offer a shuttle to Virgin Gorda.

The Baths are a must-see in Virgin Gorda. Visitors can climb and swim through the giant boulders scattered along the bay by an ancient volcano eruption.

The Spring Bay Beach, right next to The Baths, is a smaller but less popular beach, with enough boulders to make the landscape interesting.

Getting Around / Transportation

Cruisers visiting Tortola for the day will find taxis for rent at the ferry docks in Road Town. Rates are standard, but be sure to ask for the rate before getting into the cab.

The ferries are the primary form of transporting visitors from one island to another. The ferries operate by schedule, and are very affordable.

Weather / Best Times to Go

Weather is slightly cooler than the nearby St. Thomas in the U.S. Virgin Islands, which lie a bit to the southwest.

Average high temperatures are in the low to mid 80s Fahrenheit during the winter and nearly 90 during the summer.

The driest months are January through March with less than two inches of rain per month. December and April through July are a little more wet. The rainy season arrives in August and reaches a high point from September through November.

March and April are the best months to go for a combination of warm temperatures and low risk of rain. March and December are the most popular months for tourists to visit.

Cayman Islands: George Town

Western Caribbean

The Grand Cayman cruise port at George Town is one of the top five cruise stops in the Caribbean and for good reason.

About 400,000 people visit the island every year to stay at its hotels and resorts. But 1.6 million visit by cruise.

Its convenient location makes it one of the most popular western Caribbean cruise ports, and it has one of the best cruise excursions at Stingray City.

Seven Mile Beach is often named one of the best beaches in the Caribbean, and of course the capital city of George Town has plenty of duty-free shopping.

Quick Tips

- Large duty-free shopping district within walking distance of cruise docks
- Famous Seven Mile Beach also within walking distance

- The top shore excursion is Stingray City

Attractions and Shore Excursions

Stingray City easily ranks as one of the top Caribbean attractions and cruise excursions. Visitors boat out to a sandbar and jump into three feet of water with a large school of stingray that have become used to human touch. We had great fun when we did it.

The stingray don't hesitate to glide within inches -- and sometimes rub the legs -- of people in the water.

Visitors are usually given snorkeling equipment so they can see the stingray underwater. Guides will sometimes feed the stingray or even pick them up to let visitors see them up close and touch them. This is a great family experience.

Boatswain's Beach is a 23-acre marine park. It also is the home of the Cayman Turtle Centre, Grand Cayman's most popular land attraction. It is eight miles north of the cruise terminal.

It houses a research and educational facility that focuses on the conservation of sea turtles. The facilities also have predators, birds, caiman, and other creatures. Visitors can see the turtle farm by taxi, rental car or excursion bus.

Going to Hell? If you do visit this village on Grand Cayman, be sure to go to the post office like countless other tourists and send out a postcard to family or friends saying, "I've been to Hell." It is seven miles north of the cruise terminal and near the Cayman Turtle Centre.

The Queen Elizabeth II Botanic Park has 65 acres of displays, walking trail, educational exhibits, a lake and other features. The park's new

$800,000 visitor center is now the first stop on the tour.

The two-acre Heritage Garden showcases a restored early 20th-century, three-room, zinc-roofed Caymanian wooden cottage. The Floral Garden displays hundreds tropical and subtropical plants over 2.5 acres.

Nearby Beaches

The famous Seven Mile Beach is within walking distance of the cruise docks. Expect heavier crowds by the docks, so either walk farther or take a taxi to more secluded areas. There are many things to do and places to eat.

Most other beaches require access by taxi or rental car. Note that all beaches are public up to the high water mark, even beaches that front hotels and resorts.

The next closest beach to the cruise port is Smith Barcadere at South Sound. It has restrooms, picnic benches, showers and snorkeling.

Governor's beach is part of the Seven Mile Beach strip and next to the Governor's house. Cayman Falls Plaza and Governors Square plaza are by the beach and have shops, restaurants and other services.

For more remote beaches and fewer crowds, try Rum Point (40-minute drive from the docks), Kaibo (40 minutes) or Heritage (30 minutes).

Shopping / Restaurants

Visitors to the Grand Cayman cruise port can walk off their ships and start shopping and dining right away.

Most Caribbean shopping destinations offer some combination of products you can buy anywhere as well as products that are truly local. George Town is no different.

Cayman Craft Market on South Church Street has many items that are locally produced. The market is a two-minute walk south of the cruise dock. The vendors offer items of leather, thatch, wood and shell as well as traditional Caymanian food.

The Farmer's Market Cooperative is at Stacy Watler Agriculture Pavilion in Lower Valley, known as Market at the Grounds.

It is open every Saturday from 7 a.m. to 1 p.m. Visitors will find fresh produce, fish, Cayman-made products like Cayman Sea Salt, jams, preserves and hot sauces.

The Tortuga Rum Company offers 10 blends of rums, Taste of the Caribbean sections featuring samples of the Tortuga Rum Cake, Tortuga label gourmet food products and a wide variety of Caribbean speciality foods, coffees, spices and sauces.

Grand Cayman stores accept U.S. or Cayman Island dollars, travelers checks and most major credit cards.

Getting Around / Transportation

Public buses run throughout the island districts. Daily services commence at 6 a.m. and fares start at $1.50 Cayman Island dollars. Licensed buses have blue number plates and accept both U.S. and Cayman Islands dollars.

There are a few bus stops around the island, but buses can be flagged down from the side of the road.

A variety of car rental agencies are available, many of which will provide pickup at the cruise terminal.

Taxis are common at the docks; rates are fixed and should be posted. Most taxis are minivans and often require four passengers before leaving. Ask for a rate before stepping into the taxi.

Weather / Best Times to Go

The best time to visit the Grand Cayman cruise port is January through April when the average high temperature is about 87 degrees Fahrenheit. Rainfall averages less than two inches a month, according to the National Meteorological Service of the Cayman Islands.

April is the best month for warm temperatures and low risk of rain. Historically, it rains only seven days during April, which is the lowest level of any month of the year.

Otherwise, the island has heavier rain for the remaining months. Total rainfall jumps to nearly six inches in May and keeps climbing until it reaches a high point of more than eight inches in September and October.

Costa Maya: Mexico

Western Caribbean

The Costa Maya cruise port is a small but up-and-coming destination on the Caribbean coast of Mexico.

This isolated port is in the municipality of Othón P. Blanco and the state of Quintana Roo -- the same state as Cancun, Cozumel and Playa del Carmen. It lies much farther south near the border with Belize. Playa del

Carmen is a 3.5-hour drive away.

Cruise travelers are more likely to visit Costa Maya if their western Caribbean itinerary includes Belize. The port has some similar features with its sister municipalities, but it also some important differences.

Quick Tips

- The private cruise terminal is two miles from the town of Mahahual and the best beach.
- Two major commercial attractions are within walking distance of the terminal.
- Mayan ruins are major cultural attractions and shore excursions.

Attractions and Shore Excursions

Unlike the larger Cancun and Cozumel, Costa Maya was developed specifically as a cruise destination by a private company. This cruise-focused island has shops, restaurants, bars and pools. The closest nearby villages are Mahahual and Xcalak.

Mahahual lies about two miles from the cruise port, while Xcalak is about 36 miles or 92 kilometers south of the port. The port itself has a tourist shopping mall, plaza and saltwater pools.

The former fishing village at Mahanual has a boardwalk lined with hotels, restaurants, beach clubs and dive shops and beach clubs. They face white sand beaches with a shallow surf attractive to families.

Visitors can take a taxi to get there or go on excursions that include the beach as well as other water activities.

Interacting with dolphins has become a major attraction in the Caribbean, and Costa Maya is no different than other destinations. It has Dolphin Discovery, which offers a range of swimming with the dolphin packages. It is a three-minute walk south of the cruise port.

Lost Mayan is a themed water park based on a 1940s expedition. It has zip lines, pools and water slides among other features. The park is a half mile walk north of the docks.

Cruise lines offer both Dolphin Discovery and Lost Mayan as shore excursions that include transportation. Passengers who don't mind walking might want to consider buying tickets directly from the parks if it saves money.

Anyone interested in Mayan culture may want to visit Chacchoben, Kohunlich, Dzibanche and Kinichna, three archaeological sites which sit close to each other.

The most convenient Mayan excursion is about 50 minutes away at Chacchoben. It dates back to 1000 BC. The site is only partly restored, but cruise lines are promoting it more for excursion trips.

The other sites are two hours from the port, so visiting them is a full-day trip. Kohunlich is available from some cruise lines as a shore excursion.

Anyone who wants more modern activities may visit Dolphin Discovery or Lost Mayan Kingdom Adventure Park, both of which are close to the cruise terminal.

Snorkelers and scuba divers will have plenty to see at Banco Chinchorro, the largest coral atoll in the country. It is 20 miles away over the water. The atoll land is covered in mangrove while the inner lagoon has plenty of fish along with some shipwrecks.

Otherwise, cruise lines offer plenty of standard excursions such as sailing, fishing, cycling, Jeep tours and ATV tours.

Nearby Beaches

Most cruise visitors end up at Mahahual Beach, which is conveniently near the port. Mahahual Beach is often available as a shore excursion from cruise lines that include transportation.

The beach is two miles from the cruise docks right by the town of Mahahual, so visitors might combine shopping in town with a visit to the beach. Energetic people can walk the two miles; others can take a taxi or excursion bus to get there.

Other beach options include Pez Quadro Beach Club, Maya Chan Beach and Sian Ka'an. The docks have a nearby beach, but it's too rocky to swim.

Shopping / Restaurants

Costa Maya is one of the smaller cruise ports in the Caribbean because it was privately developed. The company that developed the port also invested in the town of Mahahual.

Shopping and restaurants are available in both locations, although somewhat limited compared to larger ports.

Getting Around / Transportation

Anyone who wants to go into the town of Mahahual can walk the two miles in about 40 minutes or take either a taxi or shuttle bus.

Taxi rates are set by a union, but it's a good idea to ask for the rate before getting into the cab. The recent rate for getting to Mahahual was $5.

Shops and restaurants in Mahahual are quiet in the mornings.

Weather / Best Times to Go

Like most western Caribbean cruises, Costa Maya is popular during the winter and early spring because of comfortable temperatures and low risk of rain.

The Caribbean coast of Mexico and Belize has average high temperatures in the mid-80s Fahrenheit during the winter and upper 80s to low 90s for the rest of the year.

Rainfall averages between one and three inches from January through April and reaches nine to 10 inches in September and October during the Caribbean hurricane season.

March and April are the best times to go for a combination of warm temperatures and low risk of rain.

Costa Rica: Limón

Western Caribbean

The Limón Costa Rica cruise port, or Puerto Limón, is an island of humanity surrounded by vast rain forests.

Think of it not as a cruise destination but a jumping off point for seeing Costa Rica's famous ecotourism adventures and sightseeing.

The highlight of our visit was a zip lining excursion among tall trees and chattering monkeys.

Quick Tips

- Limón city has limited tourism activities.
- The nearby national parks have the most tours and attractions.
- Know that country roads are rough; use excursion buses when possible.

Anyone visiting Puerto Limón via cruise should prepare themselves for rain. The huge volume of rain that falls on the country is why it is known for its jungles and rainforests.

But the rain also means Puerto Limón is not a place to expect sunshine and full days on the beach improving a tan and lounging in the water.

Visiting there is more about a different attitude and taking advantage of excursions and attractions that make Costa Rica a popular vacation and cruise destination.

The city itself has a small number of appealing shops, the waterfront Parque Vargas, and a local museum called Museo Etnohistoria de Limón, which is open Monday through Friday.

Playa Bonita is the nearest safe beach, located about one mile north of the city. It has a picnic area.

Otherwise, visitors take a day trip to major regional attractions.

Attractions and Shore Excursions

Major regional attractions include Cahuita, Puerto Viejo, Tortuguero National Park and Braulio Carrillo National Park.

Cahuita is 43 kilometers south of Limón and is reachable via Route 36, which mostly runs along the Caribbean coast.

It is part of the Cahuita National Park, which protects the country's largest coral reef. It's a popular spot for swimming, snorkeling and scuba diving.

Anyone with extra time might combine a Cahuita trip with Puerto Viejo, which is south of Cahuita and 58 kilometers from Limón.

Visitors can shop for handcrafted arts and crafts, drink coffee at a quiet café or feast at gourmet restaurants.

Beach goers will find good swimming along with snorkeling and diving among nearby reefs.

Tortuguero National Park, north of Limón, is one of the top ecotourism destinations in the country. Rainforest wildlife is often hard to see because of the dense vegetation.

But it is easier in Tortuguero because most of the wildlife spotting is done from quiet boats that travel along canals in the forest.

Braulio Carrillo National Park is a much farther drive at 122 kilometers. It is popular for the vast reserve of virgin forest, hiking and other adventures.

Visitors with more time on their hands may take a two-hour one-way trip to Costa Rica's capital at San Jose. The distance and travel time may discourage people with a tight schedule.

Limón Shore Excursions
LLimón has shore excursions ranging from quiet to adventurous, although here the emphasis is on adventurous.

Two of the most adventurous are zip lining, which had its start in Costa Rica, and the Aerial Tram Ride at Rainforest, a large preserve next to Braulio Carrillo National Park. For zip lining, we took the one-hour trip to Veragua Rainforest Reserve. After a safety briefing, we went over 12 different zip lines as high as 100 with exciting views of the surrounding forest, birds and monkeys.

A quieter excursion is the Tortuguero Canals with views of wildlife and numerous photo opportunities.

Other excursions include a sloth sanctuary, coffee bean plantation tour, banana plantation tour, whitewater rafting on Reventazón River and snorkeling or diving at the nearby national parks.

The whitewater rafting on Reventazón River is Class III out of I to V. That means it is moderately challenging.

Nearby Beaches

Cruise lines offer few beach excursions compared to other Caribbean destinations because there are few good beaches near Puerto Limon.

Playa Bonita is three miles north of the cruise docks. Some tours takes guests there. Otherwise, a taxi or rental car is necessary.

Cahuita National Park and Puerto Viejo are two other options. Puerto Viejo is 37 miles southeast of Puerto Limon along the coast. But Cahuita is on the way and closer, so it's better to go there.

Shopping / Restaurants

Passengers will find one of the most colorful streets in the Caribbean. Avenida 2 by the cruise docks has green, orange, blue and yellow checkers on the sidewalks. Shops and street vendors sell fresh fruit, clothing, souvenirs and other items.

Getting Around / Transportation

Costa Rica has an extensive public bus system. A bus terminal is a five-minute walk from the docks, but taxis and tourist bus companies are better options.

Several local and international car rental agencies have offices in Limón and serve the cruise port.

Weather / Best Times to Go

We visited Limón during a dry season, which means it doesn't get pounded with rain every day. Instead, on this day it was simply quite cloudy and threatening.

Average monthly rainfall ranges from a low of about six inches in September to a high of about 18 inches in July and December. It is one of the rainiest destinations in the Caribbean.

February, March, September and October are the best times to go for rain.

Temperatures maintain an average high in the mid 80s Fahrenheit and high 20s Celsius throughout most of the year.

Cozumel: San Miguel

Western Caribbean

The Cozumel cruise port at San Miguel is a standard stop for any western Caribbean cruise. It's also a chance to see one of the most popular tourist destinations in Mexico.

When we got there on a summer cruise, it was blistering hot. But that didn't stop us from enjoying the visit.

Part of what makes Cozumel so popular is the wide variety of quality experiences. Those experiences start with the ability of a cruise visitor to see either Cozumel island or take a ferry across the water to the larger city of Playa del Carmen.

Quick Tips

- San Miguel has the shopping and dining and is a long walk from the cruise terminal. Plan on taking a taxi.
- Cozumel has some of the best snorkeling and diving in the Caribbean.
- The island has several major Mayan ruins.

Attractions and Shore Excursions

One of the most popular attractions for cruise visitors to Cozumel is not on Cozumel. It's across the water at Playa del Carmen.

Visitors freely walk along a lengthy Fifth Avenue that is mostly closed to traffic. Two ferry services provide shuttles between San Miguel and Playa del Carmen. The ferry rides last about 45 minutes.

Cruise lines also offer shore excursions across the water on Mexico's mainland to major Mayan ruins at Tulum and Xcaret Eco-Archaeological Park. Passengers get to the mainland by a 45-minute ferry ride.

Tulum is the one to visit mainly for ruins. Xcaret has an underwater archaeological site, a Mayan museum, an aquarium, a butterfly pavilion, a bird-breeding aviary and swimming on lagoons, natural pools and an underground river.

All of the above excursions will take an another day and will leave little to no time for touring Cozumel.

For anyone who stays on the island, Chankanaab Park claims it is the most popular attraction on Cozumel. It has a beach, snorkeling, scuba diving, botanical garden and family entertainment. It also offers visitors a chance to interact with dolphins. Fees vary according to the experiences chosen. Many cruise lines offer a trip here as a shore excursion.

Cozumel has some modest Mayan ruins and good beaches. It also is famous for scuba diving and offers decent snorkeling. Although coral reefs are found all around the waters surrounding the island, the reefs are best on the west side.

The island has a good reputation for snorkeling, but our snorkeling excursion was not as good as others we have taken in the Caribbean. Experience shows that snorkeling is often a matter of luck with finding colorful fish and other cool sea creatures.

Cruise visitors should know that scuba diving has better coral views than snorkeling because of the depth of some of the reefs.

One benefit for divers and snorkelers alike is the quality of Cozumel beaches compared to Cancun. For that matter, any visitor to Cozumel who likes beaches should take advantage of the opportunity. Some snorkeling excursions enter the water from the beaches.

Anyone with an education interest can see the largest Mayan archaeological site on the island at San Gervasio. It was both a sacred and commercial center from 200 A.D. until the Spanish conquest.

Other Mayan sites include El Cedral, formerly the largest Mayan site on Cozumel, or Castillo Real, near the northern tip of the island.

Nearby Beaches

The largest beach near the cruise port is Chankanaab National Park Beach. It's just under four miles from the cruise terminal and requires a taxi or rental car to reach it. The park includes a lagoon, Mayan village and botanical garden.

All of the most popular beaches line the west coast with easy access for cruise visitors. A second cluster lies along the east side of the island only about five miles from the cruise dock.

If transportation isn't available from the cruise ship via a planned excursion, try taking a taxi to get to the beach. Taxi fares are standardized, but make sure to ask the driver about rates before getting into the vehicle.

We have taken taxis to Caribbean beaches and worried about getting back to the boat in time to leave. Plenty of taxis usually are available at both the cruise docks and at the major beaches. Some taxi drivers will return at pre-arranged times.

Shopping / Restaurants

Anyone who wants some hardcore shopping and dining can find plenty of it in the San Miguel cruise port. But much more is available by taking a ferry across the water to Playa del Carmen.

The Playa del Carmen shopping district on Fifth Avenue is long, packed and often festive with entertainers. It is one of our favorite shopping destinations in the Caribbean.

For those people who choose to spend the day on Cozumel, shoppers and anyone with a taste for real Mexican food can find plenty of options in the malls right by the cruise port and farther into San Miguel.

Restaurants have a heavy emphasis on local establishments with a handful of major chains such as Hard Rock Cafe. Likewise, the shopping has a strong local flavor with original arts and crafts.

Getting Around / Transportation

Cozumel has a taxi driver union with standard rates for getting around the island.

Drivers are supposed to carry a laminated rate card that they show to anyone who requests rates. Rates include zones, point to point and other information. Like anywhere else, ask for the rate before getting into the cab.

Although Cozumel has a public bus system, it does not cater to tourists.

Weather / Best Times to Go

Cozumel is popular with western Caribbean cruises from December through March because that time period is a dry season for the region. March and April are especially dry with an average of only four days of rain each month. The total rainfall is only about one inch.

Temperatures are among the warmest in the Caribbean during March and April with an average high temperature of nearly 90 degrees Fahrenheit. January and February are cooler with an average high of about 84.

Rainfall begins to climb in May and eventually reaches a high point of 10 inches a month in September and October during the peak activity of the annual Caribbean hurricane season.

Curaçao: Willemstad

Southern Caribbean

The Curaçao cruise port of Willemstad offers something special in the way of shopping and dining -- the harborfront street of Handelskade.

This UNESCO World Heritage Site is a favorite subject for photographers both in the daytime and at night when the street is brightly lit. it also fronts Punda, the city of Willemstad's main commercial district.

In addition to shopping, cruise visitors will find numerous nearby beaches -- mostly accessible via taxi -- as well as other attractions such as the Hato Caves, Curaçao Sea Aquarium and Curaçao's well-known diving and snorkeling spots.

Quick Tips

- Handelskade is famous for its picturesque waterfront.
- The harbor duty-free zone is the largest in the Caribbean.
- Most of the 17 beaches are located along the same coastline as Willemstad

Attractions and Shore Excursions

Curaçao Sea Aquarium is located on the oceanfront at Bapor Kibra. Visitors can snorkel or dive with stingray, turtles, fish and sharks among the 400 species at the facility.

Visitors can interact in the water with dolphins at the Dolphin Academy in Willemstad. Visitors experience dolphins in six different programs.

Dolphin Encounter allows them to stand on a platform in the water about waist deep, learn about the dolphins and have moderate contact with them. In Dolphin Swim, participants can swim next to dolphins and pet them.

For Dorsal Ride, two dolphins will pick up swimmers and give them rides by holding on to their dorsal fins.

In Dolphin Snorkel and Dolphin Open Water Dive, participants will dive on a reef with the dolphins. Dolphin Academy teaches participants about being a dolphin trainer.

The Hato cave covers 4,900 square meters and has limestone formations, pools, waterfalls and a Madonna statue. It is included by some cruise lines and tour operators as part of an excursion that includes a beach visit.

Nearby Beaches

The island has its fair share of beaches, but most of them aren't within walking distance of the cruise terminal. Instead, plan to get to them by taxi or excursion bus.

One example is Cabana Beach, a cruise line excursion favorite about four miles southeast of the terminal. It's also right next to the Curaçao Sea Aquarium for anyone who wants to combine both activities in one visit.

More adventurous visitors might try Curaçao's longest and whitest beach on Klein Curaçao, an uninhabited island eight miles off the southeast coast. Kenepa is one of the most popular beaches because of its two coves.

A popular choice for families is Porto Marie, which is about 18 miles or 30 kilometers from the cruise port. It's available as a four-hour excursion from some tour operators.

Many of the beaches have excellent snorkeling opportunities, especially along the Curaçao Underwater Marine Park, which lies 12 miles along the southern coast. Views include shipwrecks, expanses of hard and soft coral, and massive numbers of fish.

Shopping / Restaurants

The harbor duty free zone is a fenced area of 57 acres and the largest in the Caribbean. It is patronized by retailers from throughout the region, who come to stock up on goods from all over the world.

It's a distribution center for clothing textile, shoes, perfumes, pharmaceutical products, and many other wholesale or retail sale goods with attractive duty free prices.

Most of the companies in the zone distribute products from the United States, Europe, and Asia to the Caribbean and Latin America. There is also tax-free shopping at the free zone.

Goods purchased in the zone must be shipped directly to your home or transferred to your ship or flight. You can pick them up when you arrive home. The city's commercial center, Punda, has numerous shops offering everything from clothing to jewelry and souvenirs. Many little shops sell electronics, souvenirs, and cheaper clothing.

Opening hours may vary, but most shops are open from Monday till Saturday from 8.30 a.m. to 12 p.m. and from 2 p.m. to 6 p.m. At official holidays all shops and banks are closed.

Many shops in the center of Willemstad are open on Sundays if a big cruise ship has docked at the harbor.

Most shops accept U.S. dollars and international credit cards, and in some shops you can also pay with your regular bank card. Prices are fixed and most of the time it's not possible to return or change purchased goods.

Renaissance Mall and Rif Fort has 50 stores with world and local brands. Goods include fashion, accessories, fragrances, jewelry and souvenirs. The mall also has 15 restaurants and bars.

It is downtown in the Renaissance Curaçao Resort next to the pontoon bridge in Otrobanda. Free parking is on site.

Getting Around / Transportation

The island has two kinds of public transportation -- large yellow or blue buses, which are called Konvooi and go for a longer distance, and on most urban routes there are collective cars or vans, similar to taxis. They have BUS on their registration plates.

The major bus terminals are located outside the postal office at the Waaigat in Punda and next to the underpass in Otrobanda.

The large buses cover 12 routes departing from the Punda terminal and nine routes departing from Otrobanda. The routes reach most areas of the island.

Most city buses go once every hour and every two hours a bus goes westwards, less frequent on Sundays.

Nearly a dozen car rental agencies are available on the island. Most are concentrated at the airport, but Budget has four locations in resorts near Willemstad. Most agencies offer pick up and drop off.

Weather / Best Times to Go

Curaçao weather is much like the weather of nearby Aruba: dry and hot most of the year.

Rainfall averages about one inch a month from January through September and more than three inches a month from October through December. It reaches the lowest point of the year of less than one inch from March through June.

The average high temperature reaches about 90 degrees Fahrenheit in June and stays there until October. Winter high temperatures stay in the mid 80s Fahrenheit. The best months to visit are March through June for a combination of warm temperatures and low risk of rain.

Dominica: Roseau

Eastern Caribbean

The Dominica cruise port of Roseau is modest by Caribbean standards, but it also is a gateway to one of the region's best eco tourism islands.

Dominica is unlike almost any other island that mainstream cruise lines visit. It is dense with rainforests, waterfalls, and fresh fruit. For an idea of what to expect, watch the "Pirates of the Caribbean" movie, which was filmed in part on the island.

Rainforest covers two thirds of this 464-square-mile island, nicknamed "The Nature Island". Dominica is home to more than 1,200 different plant species and only 70,000 people.

Cruisers visiting the island for only a day should plan on activities much different than most Caribbean islands.

Most cruise lines dock at the Roseau Cruise Ship Berth. Visitors will walk off the ships and right into the tourism district. They will find a small district than other major ports.

Quick Tips

- Hiking is the most popular attraction on this wet, eco tourism island.
- Beaches are rarer than most islands and often rocky.
- Dominica is one of the wettest islands in the Caribbean.

Attractions and Shore Excursions

Cruise passengers may find that the port of Roseau has a small but decent tourism district. Otherwise, the city has few major attractions. The big attractions on this wet and rainy island are the rivers and waterfalls.

One worthy attraction in the city is the Dominica Botanic Gardens, which are less than 10 minutes away by foot along King George V Street from the cruise terminal. The botanical gardens stretch over 40 acres and display more than 50 types of plants and trees.

The most popular shore excursions on the island are hiking, swimming and river tubing. Most of the hikes travel through the rainforest and have levels of difficulty by category.

Tubing on the Layou River is a way for the whole family to enjoy Dominica's beautiful scenery. Several companies and guides offer river tubing. Visitors can hire them through their cruise line or directly right along the cruise port.

Guides are available for a hike to Boiling Lake. This eight-hour round trip hike takes visitors to a water-filled crater, said to reach 197 degrees Fahrenheit.

Dominica's national parks are all worth visiting. Morne Diablotin National Park offers the highest point in the island, rising more than 5,000 feet above sea level. The Cabrits National Park is an old fort of the Royal Navy in the Caribbean. Visiting national sites cost $5 each or $12 for a week-long pass.

The Rainforest Tram offers a view of the rainforest without the strenuous hiking. Ziplining is also available along the Layou, Dominica's longest river. The cruise port is the starting point for many other day trips and excursions, from biking to canoeing to horseback riding.

Passengers can finish the day with an ice cream or freshly picked vegetable from Roseau's main market.

Nearby Beaches

Dominica is a great place to go for ecotourism adventures such as hiking and whitewater rafting. It isn't the place to go for beaches because they are mostly rocky from past volcanic activity.

Cruise lines and tour operators don't offer any beach excursions. Still, one of the better options is the black sand Mero Beach in the village of Mero. It is 12 miles north of the Roseau cruise port. Cruise visitors will need a taxi or rental car to get there.

Shopping / Restaurants

Shopping and dining in Roseau take a back seat to the natural attractions.

The heart of downtown Roseau is just yards away from the cruise port. Roseau is said to offer the best fruit and vegetable market in the Caribbean.

The city has a modest tourist district with shops, art and craft stands, and restaurants. Several restaurants offer Creole cuisine, including Pearl's Restaurant on 50 King George V Street (767-448-8707), and La Robe Creole, located on Victoria Street (767-448-2896).

On my last visit, I walked from the tourist district to the other side of the city and back again. I saw few tourists outside of the tourist district.

Getting Around / Transportation

Taxis line up along the port, offering rides to travelers. Taxis offer a tour of the island and will usually charge $150. Most excursion operators arrive and leave from there as well.

Taxis have H, HA or HB starting the registration numbers on the license plates. Bus service is available from private operators.

Just steps past the taxis are car rentals for cruisers who want to explore the island independently. Cars drive on the left side of the road because of the island's British colonial history. A note of caution: the roads in Dominica are often narrow and difficult to navigate. Excursion buses are a safer and better option.

Weather / Best Times to Go

Dominica has an average year-round temperature of 77 degrees Fahrenheit. The island has a rainforest climate, and receives, on average, 197 inches of rain per year.

The driest months of the year are January through April, but short, midday showers are still common.

Dominica is a rainforest island because it receives a great deal of rain throughout the year. It is one of the wettest islands in the Caribbean.

The average monthly rainfall is four to six inches from January through April during the dry season. Dominica's dry season is as wet as the rainy season for most Caribbean islands.

Average rainfall jumps to nine inches in May and backs off a bit in June. It then starts climbing again until it reaches a high point of about 15 inches in November. The best time to go to Dominica is April for a combination of low risk of rain and warmer temperatures. The worst time to go is any month from late fall until early winter.

Dominican Republic: Amber Cove

Eastern Caribbean

The filming location of the original Jurassic Park movie has become an $85 million port for Carnival Cruise Lines.

Amber Cove is a small bay near the resort city of Puerto Plata on the north coast of Dominican Republic. It lies just south of Grand Turk and the Turks and Caicos islands.

The port officially opened in October 2015 with the arrival of Carnival Victory and 3,000 passengers. It highlights the return of the first cruise passengers to Puerto Plata in 30 years.

The strategic location of the port will potentially result in future cruise stops in Cuba, Carnival says.

Other Carnival brands will visit the port including Cunard, P&O, AIDA, Azura, Costa and Holland America.

Quick Tips

- Ocean World animal park is the largest nearby attraction.
- Nearby Puerto Plata offers the most shopping and dining.
- Excursion buses are a better deal than taxis for reaching Puerto Plata.

Attractions and Shore Excursions

Amber Cove represents another step in a trend toward cruise lines developing their own ports and providing attractions that encourage visitors to stay on site or nearby.

They also provide an opportunity for the cruise lines to become excursion operators for anyone wanting more adventurous activities.

Amber Cove has a welcome center with a crafts marketplace, restaurants, pool, splash zone and green space areas.

"The new port will host one of the most extensive shore excursion programs available in the Caribbean, offering roughly 40 different landside experiences including beaches, water sports and special culinary, cultural and adventure options," Carnival says.

One of the largest nearby attractions is Ocean World, a two-mile drive from the port. Ocean World has animal encounters with an emphasis on swimming with dolphins.

Puerto Plata with much more shopping and dining lies seven miles southeast of the port. The town was founded by Christopher Columbus and was the first European settlement in the Americas.

Just before reaching Puerto Plata, visitors may want to see Fort San Felipe. The fort, completed in 1577, was built to protect the city from pirates.

The Amber Cove port has various shore and water excursions that are standard for Caribbean destinations. They include ATV rides, snorkeling and boating trips. But it also has a major national park that has some unique features.

Parque Nacional Isabel De Torres is located about the same distance from Amber Cove as Puerto Plata, although just south of the city.

The main feature of the park is Mount Isabel De Torres. The 2,600-foot mountain is known for its cable ride to the top and panoramic views of

Puerto Plata, Christ the Redeemer statue and the surrounding countryside. The park also has hiking trails, botanical gardens and a bird sanctuary.

Nearby Beaches

Anyone who wants a more authentic beach than the one at Amber Cove can venture three plus miles by taxi or rental car to calm Cofresi Beach. It is next to Water World Adventure Park, which makes it easy to combine both activities in one trip.

The rougher waters of Grand Beach or Playa Grande are four miles in the other direction. Otherwise, good options that take up to an hour to reach are Sosua Beach and Cabarete Beach. Both of them are in attractive tourist towns to the east of Puerto Plata. Some cruise line excursions do go to Cabarete.

Shopping / Restaurants

Amber Cove's location near Puerto Plata leaves shoppers with two choices. Anyone who wants to do some quick shopping can do it at the Carnival Cruise Line shops at Amber Cove. Anyone who wants some serious shopping with many more options should take the short trip over to Puerto Plata.

Carnival offered one shopping excursion into Puerto Plata at the time of this writing. It included some sightseeing and a stop for shopping at Puerto Plata Parque Central, otherwise known as Central Park.

The park has quite a few shops and restaurants as well as several historical attractions including St. Philip the Apostle Cathedral and the House of Culture.

Getting Around / Transportation

Attractions around Amber Cove such as beaches, Puerto Plata and Parque Nacional Isabel De Torres are close enough to tempt some people to rent a car.

Car rentals are available at the Amber Cove docks as well as taxis. A one-way trip to Puerto Plata costs about $35. Rental car agencies such as Alamo and National have an office at the cruise port.

Weather / Best Time to Go

The dry season for Amber Cove is June through September and part of October. The heaviest rains historically take place from November through January, according to the Dominican Republic National Meteorological Office.

Average high temperatures reach 90 degrees Fahrenheit or 32 degrees Celsius during the summer. They decline to about 84 degrees Fahrenheit or 29 degrees Celsius during the winter.

Dominican Republic: La Romana

Eastern Caribbean

La Romana is Dominican Republic's third largest city and the most popular cruise port in this country that shares an island with Haiti.

It is especially popular with Carnival cruise ships because the company built the port.

Cruise visitors may find that the main attraction in La Romana is the resort village of Casa de Campo, a 7,000-acre complex that features golf, tennis, skeet shooting, equestrian, beaches and more. It is accessible from cruise ships via taxis and excursion buses.

Like other major destinations in Dominican Republic such as Punta Cana and Puerto Plata, La Romana is a destination that emphasizes plenty of activities in confined areas.

Quick Facts

- The main attraction is the resort village of Casa de Campo
- Facilities at the cruise dock are limited
- Almost all activities require transportation via excursion operators

Attractions and Shore Excursions

Several beaches are near the cruise docks and accessible by shuttle or taxi depending on the location. They include Casa de Campo, Isla Catalina and a 10-minute taxi ride to Bayahibe Beach.

Saona Island is accessible by boat from Bayahibe and is popular for its beaches and excursions on catamarans and speedboats. Lucky tourists will be joined by dolphins that swim and leap nearby.

The region's most popular cultural attraction is Altos de Chavón, a 15th century artists' village located next to Casa de Campo. It has hosted performers such as Frank Sinatra, Santana, Sting, Plácido Domingo, Andrea Bocelli, Heart and Air Supply, according to the Dominican Republic Ministry of Tourism.

The village was designed by former Paramount movies set designer

Roberto Copa. He also created movie sets for famous Italian film director Federico Fellini.

Snorkelers and divers will want to visit the Guadalupe underwater museum, which can also be seen by snorkeling above it.

Another popular spot is the living museum of the Cara Merchant shipwreck, which once belonged to the famous Captain Kidd who was sentenced to death after being accused of being a pirate.

A marine coral reef nature preserve surrounds the six-square-mile Isla Catalina, which attracts thousands of divers and snorkelers each year.

For anyone willing to take the time, Carnival offers a one-hour ride to Punta Cana for the Dolphin Island Park and dolphin encounters.

Another one-hour excursion drive will go to Hoyo Azul Cave. This natural pool with crystal clear blue water is at the base of a giant cliff. The excursion also includes educational trails and animal encounters.

For golfers, Teeth of the Dog designed by Pete Dye has been called the top golf course in the Caribbean and among the top 100 in the world ranked by Golf Magazine. It is located at the Casa de Campo resort. The resort also has art galleries that display painters and sculptures from around the Dominican Republic. Three other nearby Dye-designed courses are Dye Fore, The Links, and La Romana Country Club. Another option is La Estancia, designed by his son, P. B. Dye.

Nearby Beaches

Two of the best beach options for anyone taking a taxi are Playa El Caleton and Playa Bayahibe. El Caleton is close and decent. Bayahibe is farther and better.

Playa El Caleton is just less than two miles from the cruise terminal and a better choice for anyone who wants a quick visit. Bayahibe is a 25-minute drive and has more to offer. It's also often available as a cruise excursion.

Two smaller options are Playa Caleta at five miles and Playa El Minitas at four miles from the terminal.

Shopping / Restaurants

Altos de Chavón has a small number of shops and restaurants. Another shopping and dining option is The Marina, a village within Casa de Campo.

Getting Around / Transportation

Shuttles and taxis line up at the docks to take visitors to Casa de Campo, the Marina and Altos de Chavon. Taxi rates are often negotiable.

Weather / Best Times to Go

La Romana and other locations in the Dominican Republic are blessed with warmer weather than average temperatures in the Caribbean throughout the year.

Daily highs average in the mid to upper 80s Fahrenheit and break 90 degrees from June through September. Rainfall is lowest during this time as well. The worst time to visit is November and December when average rainfall reaches nine inches a month. La Romana also has a brief rainy season in May.

Grenada: St. George's

Eastern Caribbean

A Grenada cruise visit falls in the same league as Dominica, Jamaica and other island nations known for their mountains, lush rainforests and waterfalls.

Cruise ships and resort visitors don't necessarily go there just for the beaches. They go there as much as anything for the beauty and eco tourism.

The "Isle of Spice" consists of the main island of Grenada and the smaller islands of Carriacou and Petite Martinique. It is not the most popular Caribbean island, but it does have some unique qualities that attract cruise and resort visitors alike.

Cruise ships dock at the Grenada Port Authority cruise ship terminal. Passengers will walk off the docks and into St. George's. Grenada's capital has a horseshoe-shaped harbor surrounded by multi-colored dockside warehouses and the red-tiled roofs of shops and homes.

The city is filled with English, French and West Indian history and also has many options to view French and British Colonial architecture.

Quick Tips

- Old military forts make up the most important historical attractions.
- Hiking and waterfalls are popular natural attractions.
- Grand Anse is a must-see beach.

Attractions and Shore Excursions

Attractions in St. George's for walking tours include the Grenada National Museum on Young Street near Vendors Market. It is in an old army barracks and prison built in 1704.

Grenada is one of the better island destinations in the Caribbean for old military forts. Shore excursions from cruise lines include them in tours of the island.

Fort George, built in 1705, is less than a half mile from the cruise terminal. It has excellent views of the city and the harbor. It is still in use as a police headquarters. Its battery of old cannons are still in use during special ceremonies.

Fort Frederick is better preserved, but it is two miles outside of the city. Like Fort George, it has 360-degree views of St. George's and Grenada.

Otherwise, Grenada's tourist attractions are mainly outdoors and created by nature. The main island has many hiking opportunities and quite a few waterfalls.

Annandale Falls are easily accessible from St. George's. It has restrooms and nearby shops. Concord Valley has three waterfalls known together as the Concord Falls is three falls together in the Concord Valley.

Fontainebleau has a waterfall dropping off a 65-foot cliff into a clear pool. The Royal Mt. Carmel Falls have two that drop more than 70 feet.

Tours include the Grenada Sugar Factory in St. George's, the River Antoine Rum Distillery in St. Patrick parish, Westerhall Rum Distillery in St. David and Grenville Nutmeg Processing Station in St. Andrew.

Tours near the St. John parish include Dunfermline Rum Distillery,

Douglaston Spice Estate and Gouyave Nutmeg Processing Station.

Beaches

The best beach on Grenada and one of the closest to the St. George's cruise port is Grand Anse Beach. It has a reputation as one of the best beaches in the world by top travel writers and critics.

Grand Anse Beach is two miles of white sand in a sheltered bay and is a favorite of many locals and visitors alike. It is four miles or 20 minutes south of the cruise terminal over a slow road.

Grand Anse is heavily featured in advertisements about the island, and several major hotels are located next to it. Indeed, the beach has a lot to offer, from water sports and scuba diving shops, to the vendors markets with local crafts and several wonderful restaurants.

Morne Rouge Bay is an option for anyone who wants a smaller and more secluded beach with calmer waters. It is only one miles south of the Grand Anse beach.

Shopping / Restaurants

St. George's is one of the less-visited cruise ports in the Caribbean, and the small cruise terminal reflects the number of visitors. But the streets of St. George's make up for the difference with souvenir shops, restaurants and art galleries.

Esplanade Mall on St. Juilles Street, less than a half mile north of the cruise terminal, is the only shopping mall in St. George's. It has about 50 shops covering the usual range of duty-free goods such as jewelry, clothing, perfumes and crafts.

The open-air Market Square on Young Street is a closer option at a quarter of a mile east of the cruise terminal. It may not appeal to cruise visitors as much because it has quite a bit of fresh produce that can't go back on the ship. Daring visitors can eat their lunches right there. It's colorful, lively and has some crafts for sale.

Visitors to Grand Anse Beach can go to Spiceland Mall, which has about 20 shops, or Vendors Market, which has about 80 booths with arts, crafts, spices, produce and other goods for sale.

Getting Around / Transportation

Land and water taxis also are available for hire. Hotel and airport taxis have fixed rates, while rates vary for other points of interest around the island. Always ask for the rate before getting into the taxi.

Rental car drivers must be at least 25 years old, have a valid driver's license and get a $60 EC driving permit from the police station at The Carenage in St Georges. Some rental agencies provide the permit.

The island has a public bus system that runs between 6 a.m. and 9 p.m. Monday through Saturday, according to the Grenada Tourism Authority. Each bus has a zone sticker in the front and a conductor to help passengers. Fares cost between $2.50 and $6.50 EC.

Weather / Best Time to Go

Grenada is one of the warmer islands in the Caribbean with an average high temperature of about 86 degrees Fahrenheit or 30 Celsius almost year round.

The dry season is February through May with an average rainfall of one inch or less. The rainy season begins in June. Total rainfall keeps climbing until it reaches more than 10 inches historically in November.

The most popular month to visit is August followed by December, according to the Caribbean Tourism Organization. The least popular is September and then a tie between June and October.

Even though August is the most popular month to visit, May is better because of a low risk of rain.

Guadeloupe: Pointe-à-Pitre

Eastern Caribbean

Guadeloupe in the Leeward Islands is getting more and more traffic from cruise ships in recent years.

The island, still technically a part of France, is rich with French influence, from the language to the currency.

Some English is spoken, especially in the major tourist areas. But having a French dictionary on hand is helpful in some locations.

Guadeloupe is unique in the Caribbean for having five harbors that can welcome cruise ships.

The main cruise port is at the Centre Saint-John Perse terminal in Guadeloupe's central city, Pointe-à-Pitre.

This city of 16,000 sits on Grande Terre near the sea channel that separates it from Basse-Terre. The central location makes it easier for visitors to explore both halves of The Butterfly Island.

Quick Tips

- The best attractions are outside of the city.
- Grande Anse is the island's best and most famous beach.
- January through March are the best months to visit for low risk of rain.

Attractions and Shore Excursions

Stretching 629 square miles, Guadeloupe is packed with things to do and see. The island is unusual in that it is an archipelago of two distinct halves in the shape of a butterfly.

They are Grande-Terre in the east and Basse-Terre in the west. For this reason, Guadeloupe has the nickname of The Butterfly Island.

Deciding what to do before arriving will ease the overwhelming sensation many cruisers experience when coming ashore.

The cruise port at Pointe-à-Pitre offers the usual port shopping plus some interesting historical attractions.

Visitors can see colonial buildings such as Marché Saint-Antoine or Place de la Victoire. Other noteworthy historical sites include St-Paul Church and the brightly colored district of La Darse, which has Creole houses in the style of New Orleans.

Musée St-John Perse near Place de la Victoire is a three-level museum dedicated to Alexis Leger (1887–1975), a French poet, diplomat and winner of the Nobel Prize in Literature. Leger, who went by the name of Saint-John Perse, was born in Guadeloupe and spent his first 12 years there. The 19th century building is an example of a period Creole home and has displays of Leger's life and work.

Visitors wanting to stay on foot may enjoy the outdoor markets in Pointe-à-Pitre, which sell food, spices, and potpourri.

The local food in Guadeloupe is a mix of French and creole influences and can be purchased at the outdoor markets.

Natural attractions and adventures are common outside of Pointe-à-Pitre.

Cruisers wanting to see as much of Guadeloupe as possible without exhausting themselves may want to go on a land tour to see a large part of the island.

The tour takes travelers through fields and past beaches to show them the wide diversity of Guadeloupe. The tour makes several stops along the way to allow travelers to get out and look around.

Basse-Terre, which is the eastern half of The Butterfly Island, is a part of Guadeloupe populated with waterfalls, rivers, and volcanoes.

Several tourism companies offer round trips to the Trois Cornes Waterfalls. Round trips are usually based on group rates, and cost around $100.

La Soufriere is a 4,813-foot-high active volcano located in Basse-Terre. This volcano is part of the National Park of Guadeloupe. Visitors can drive most of the way up the volcano and then can hike to the very top. This excursion takes about two hours.

Karukeraland Adventure and Water Park has slides, the Fun Gliss and Mango Splash, a pool, the paddling pool and the fountains. It also has a wildlife park with more than 200 exotic animals such as swans, peacocks, llamas, ponies and goats. The park is about 40 minutes east of the cruise port.

Nearby Beaches

Guadeloupe is not known for good beaches near the cruise port. To get to a decent beach, cruisers will likely have to take a taxi, excursions bus or another form of public transportation.

Taxis are not metered, so travelers should set a price before getting in the cab.

The most famous beach for visitors to Pointe-à-Pitre is Grande Anse on the northwest coast of the island. It is 45 minutes away by car.

For snorkelers and water sport enthusiasts, northern Basse-Terre's shoreline is brimming with underwater life.

Ferries can also be taken to Pigeon Island from Pointe-à-Pitre.
A sail and snorkel tour takes visitors to Grand Cul de Sac Marin, part of the Guadeloupe National Park, for a day long adventure on the water.

Shopping / Restaurants

The streets surrounding the cruise terminal have enough shops to satisfy cruise browsers.

For a more compact experience, Place de la Victoire is a good start point for shopping and restaurants. It is a quarter of a mile from the cruise terminal along the waterfront. It has the Central Market among other shopping and dining attractions.

Destreland in Point-a-Pitre is the largest shopping mall in Guadeloupe, but it is five miles from the cruise terminal.

Getting Around / Transportation

All major international rental car companies have a presence in Guadeloupe. The Guadeloupe Islands Tourist Board recommends renting a car as the best way to get around the island.

Taxi rates are set by the government, but drivers don't always follow the rates. Check for a meter and settle on a rate before getting into the taxi. Look for a "Friendly Taxi" logo on the vehicle or driver, the tourist board says.

The main island has an extensive bus service, but travelers will finding that knowing the French language will make the system easier to use.

Weather / Best Time to Go

Guadeloupe is a rainy island with a dry season from January through March. The average rainfall then is about three inches a month.

Rainfall picks up in June and keeps climbing until it averages about nine inches a month from September through November.

Average high temperatures stay in the mid to upper 80s Fahrenheit and upper 20s Celsius throughout the year.

January through March are the best times to visit for a combination of warm temperatures and low risk of rain. June has a slight break in rain and warmer temperatures.

Havana: Cuba

Western Caribbean

Havana Cuba has skyrocketed into popularity among cruise destinations in the Caribbean thanks to better diplomatic relations between Cuba and the United States.

A handful of cruises began visiting the Havana port after the death in late 2016 of Cuban dictator Fidel Castro. Cruise sites are now filled with options for visiting historic Havana.

And history indeed is the highlight of a Havana cruise. Cuba is known for the revolution that brought Castro to power in 1959. But the island and especially Havana are packed with colonial history including Old San Juan, which dates back to the 1500s.

Quick Tips

- Old Havana is a major historical attraction.
- Beaches are hard to reach.
- Late spring is the best time to go.

Attractions and Shore Excursions

Old Havana evokes comparisons to Old San Juan. The city dates back to 1519 as a settlement for Spanish conquerors. They used the city as a center of trade, a strategic military position and storage for treasures brought back from the New World before transport back to Spain. A seawall begun in the 17th century took 100 years to complete, according to the Cuba Tourist Board.

One of the major attractions within Old Havana is Cathedral Square, which is made up of Plaza Vieja (Old Square) and Francis of Assisi square. Plaza Vieja is the location of the San Juan de Jaruco mansion. Francis of Assisi square has a church and convent of the same name. The Museum of Sacred Art is located in the convent's cloisters.

The Castillo de la Real Fuerza, built in 1577, displays the most important pottery collection in Cuba. La Giraldilla, an artistic wind vane and symbol of the city, sits atop the building. Other attractions in the square are the Captain-General's Palace (Museum of the City) and El Segundo Cabo.

Museo Nacional de Bellas Artes de La Habana in Old Havana exhibits Cuban art collections from the colonial era to current times.

Military buffs can explore the Morro-Cabaña park, which showcases two major ruins in one historical fortress.The Castle of the Three Kings of El Morro was erected in 1630. The fortress of San Carlos de la Cabaña was built in 1774. Both structures contain military museums.

Visitors to the park also will be able to see Prado Promenade, the Great Theatre of Havana and the Capitol building. The Capitol building has the Statue of the Republic, which has a diamond planted at its feet to mark kilometer zero of Central Road.

Malecón is a broad ocean-side road that extends for five miles along the city's beach. It starts at the mouth of Havana Harbor by Old Havana and ends in the Vedado neighborhood. The boardwalk is especially popular with walkers and fishermen.

Malecón offers access to other nearby attractions including the Revolution Square, University of Havana, the José Martí Monument and the Colon Cemetery, which is one of the world's largest necropolises.

Napoleon Museum, located by the University of Havana, is a major collection of art and other items from the 18th and 19th centuries. It contains almost 8,000 items, most of them originating between the French Revolution and the Second Empire.

Revolution Square or Plaza de la Revolución is one of the largest city squares in the world and the location of many major political rallies and speeches by former president Fidel Castro. Overlooking the square is José Martí Memorial with a 358-foot tower and a 59-foot statue. Many government ministries surround the square.

The fishing village of Cojimar is about three miles east of Havana. It is famous with tourists because Ernest Hemingway, a winner of the Nobel prize for literature, kept his boat there, developed material for many of his stories and found the inspiration for his classic novel "The Old Man and the Sea."

Nearby Beaches

Havana is not known for major beaches that are easy to reach for cruise visitors. Cruise lines and tour operators offer few excursions if any to nearby beaches.

Playa del Este, 10 miles east of Havana, is the Riviera of Cuba with more than nine miles of beaches and hotels located between Bacuranao and Guanabo. It is part of a string of beaches on a strip known as Santa María del Mar. If an excursion isn't available, the next option for getting there is a taxi.

Weather / Best Time to Go

Havana's monthly weather has is not quite as warm as many other destinations in the Caribbean. Although predictably warm for most of the year, the city has spikes of rainfall in June and October.

Late spring is the best time to visit for a combination of warm temperatures and low risk of rain. April historically is the best month of the year for weather.

The average high temperature in Havana ranges from 78 degrees Fahrenheit and 26 degrees Celsius in January to 89 degrees F and 32 degrees C during the peak of summer in August, according to the Cuba Institute of Meteorology.

Rainfall in Havana reaches a high point of more than seven inches in June. It declines for several months until it hits another high point of more than seven inches in October.

The city clearly has a dry season that runs from December through April every year when total rainfall each month averages less than three inches. May, November and August hover right around three and a half to four inches.

Rain days, or the average number of days that it rains each month, is lower in Havana than most other Caribbean locations.

June, September and October average 10 to 11 days each, while March and April average only three days each.

The month with the highest average temperature and lowest rainfall is August, when the high reaches 89 degrees Fahrenheit and rainfall totals 3.9 inches.

Jamaica: Falmouth

Eastern Caribbean

"Historic Falmouth Cruise Port" is a 32-acre cruise terminal and park developed by the Jamaica Port Authority and Royal Caribbean Cruise Line. The development includes a craft market, duty-free and boutique shops, restaurants, offices and homes within walking distance.

Falmouth was founded in 1769 and is considered one of the Western Hemisphere's best-preserved towns from the Georgian era.

Quick Tips

- Montego Bay and Dunn's River Falls are popular cruise excursions.
- Beaches usually require a taxi or other transportation to reach them.
- The best time to go for weather is March or especially April.

Attractions and Shore Excursions

The Falmouth cruise port emphasizes local history and cultural. Beyond the port, many of the major attractions lie to the east near Ocho Rios or to the west at Montego Bay. Ocho Rios is about an hour away by car or tour bus, while Montego Bay is about 45 minutes away.

Dunn's River Falls near Ocho Rios is an hour away. The cascading waterfalls allow visitors to climb up them in a daisy chain. They are a popular shore excursion from the Falmouth cruise port.

The Rainforest Adventures Park at Mystic Mountain near Dunn's River

Falls also is about a one-hour drive. It offers bobsledding, ziplines and "tranopy" tours.

Dolphin lovers can go to Dolphin Cove near Montego Bay to swim with them. But it is an hour and 20 minutes by car or bus to the east of Falmouth because it is on the far side of Montego Bay. Dunn's River Falls is a quicker drive.

Within Falmouth, an easy way to discover the local history is via a trolley tour.

One of the more significant historical buildings in Falmouth is the William Knibb Memorial Baptist Church. It was built by a missionary and leader in the movement to abolish slavery in Jamaica.

Luminous Lagoon is marshland between Falmouth and the town of Rock. It is home to millions of dinoflagellates, microscopic organisms that produce an eerie glow at night. They reveal outlines of fish and other objects in the water.

Rafting, kayaking and water tubing on Rio Bueno and Martha Brae rivers are common excursions for recreational cruise visitors.

Rose Hall Great House near Montego Bay is a chance to visit the home of the "white witch of Rose House". Visitors can hear a few horror stories to chill the bones under a hot Jamaican sun. The house is about 20 minutes from the Falmouth cruise docks.

Nearby Beaches

Burwood Beach is a public beach about four miles east of the cruise port. Visitors will need a taxi to get there.

Some cruise excursions offer visits to Doctor's Cave Beach, which is near Montego Bay about 40 minutes from the Falmouth docks.

Shopping / Restaurants

The Port of Falmouth has a variety of retail and duty free shops, restaurants and excursion operators in 120,000 square feet of retail space.

Shops sell the usual range of products in developed Caribbean tourism districts including duty-free jewelry, clothing, electronics, perfume, arts, crafts and souvenirs.

Restaurants at the port facility include Margaritaville, Starbucks, DQ, Quiznos, Nathan's Famous, Auntie Anne's and Patty Port.

Weather / Best Times to Go

Falmouth has some of the lowest risk of rain among all of the cruise ports in the Caribbean.

Like most Caribbean destinations, it has a dry season from January through April when the average rainfall is two to three inches a month, according to the Meteorological Service of Jamaica.

That total increases to four inches from May through August and then climbs to five inches in September and six inches in October. Average monthly rainfall declines again to four inches in November and December.

Temperatures hover in a narrow range throughout most of the year. The average daytime temperatures range from the low 80s Fahrenheit in the winter to the high 80s in the summer.

Jamaica: Montego Bay

Western Caribbean

Montego Bay, Jamaica, is a western Caribbean cruise port and the tourism capital of Jamaica.

The second largest city on the island is a hub for many visitors to Jamaica. Besides a cruise terminal, the city also has the Sangster International Airport.

It is the flight destination for anyone planning to stay in hotels or resorts for Montego Bay, Negril and Ocho Rios, among other locations. Sangster is only 70 minutes by air from Miami, FL.

Cruise ships often come to Montego Bay from embarkation ports such as Tampa, New Orleans and Galveston and continue on to Grand Cayman and Cozumel.

Quick Tips

- Mystic Mountain and Dolphin Cove are two major attractions.
- Beaches require transportation to reach them.
- April and July are two of the best months for weather.

Attractions and Shore Excursions

Cruise visitors will have shore excursions ranging from Jamaican bobsledding to bamboo rafting, ziplining, kayaking, waterfalls, beaches and dolphin swims.

Mystic Mountain is an entertainment complex 90 minutes east of the cruise port that offers "bobsledding", zip lining and other activities in one package. Despite the distance, it is a common cruise shore excursion.

Adventurous cruise visitors can raft and kayak on the mild Great River. They take excursion buses inland to the starting point, drift down river toward the ocean and reach Great River Bay about seven miles south of the cruise port.

Like many Caribbean cruise destinations, Montego Bay has an attraction where visitors can swim and interact with dolphins. Dolphin Cove is 18 miles west of the cruise docks.

Rose Hall Great House is a chance to visit the home of the "white witch of Rose House" and hear a few horror stories to chill the bones under a hot Jamaican sun.

The Georgian mansion is an 18th century plantation home that was refurbished in the 1960s. Decor and furnishings reflect the 18th century lifestyle. Tropical gardens add a bonus for visitors.

Nearby Beaches

Some of the better beaches are on resort properties.

The city has plenty of nearby beaches with at least nine of them within five miles of the cruise port. Dump-Up Beach and Events Park is right in the city and often crowded. Belvedere, Cornwall, Doctor's Cave and Walter Fletcher beaches are a mile or less away from downtown.

Doctor's Cave Beach is located on Montego Bay, in the northwest section of Jamaica. This pretty beach has more to offer its visitors than fine white sand.

Doctor's Cave beach is arguably one of the best locations on the island for exploring the world underneath the crystal clear water.

Aqua Sol Theme Park a few miles north of the cruise docks is mostly just a beach with an entrance fee rather than a park.

Otherwise, cruise line shore excursions to beaches often take passengers to resort beaches for the sake of a better overall experience.

Shopping / Restaurants

The closest shopping to the cruise docks is at Montego Freeport, which is a brief walk straight south.

Many-free shops are at the City Centre Shopping Mall, which is two and a half miles north of the docks. It is right by the Aqua Sol Theme Park and Dump Up Beach and Events Park.

Look for the nearby Old Fort Craft Park, which is a robust arts and crafts market. Shoppers at each place should be prepared for aggressive vendors.

Getting Around / Transportation

Some Caribbean cruise ports have great public transportation. Others do not. Montego Bay falls in the second category.

Taxi drivers in Montego Bay do not have the best reputation. Rates are metered. Be sure to ask for the rate before getting into the cab.

Possibly the best option for getting around is with cruise excursion buses. Although a cruise excursion is sometimes more expensive than taking a taxi, it's worth considering for Montego Bay visitors.

Weather / Best Times to Go

Any month is a good time for weather in Montego Bay except for a short rainy season in May and a heavier rainy season in August, September and October caused by the annual Caribbean hurricane season.

Rainfall averages one to three inches a month from January through April and again in July, according to the Meteorological Service of Jamaica. It's at least four inches during the other months of the year and reaches a high point of nearly seven inches in October.

The average high temperature is 88 degrees Fahrenheit or about 31 Celsius during the summer months. The averages high stay in the low 80s Fahrenheit or upper 20s Celsius during the winter.

The best months to go for a combination of warm temperatures and low risk of rain are April and July. These recommendations are based on long-term weather patterns and may vary from year to year.

Jamaica: Ocho Rios

Western Caribbean

Ocho Rios cruise port visitors will find it is one of the best destinations for attractions and things to do on the island of Jamaica.

The town is a popular cruise port as well as a popular all-inclusive resort destination. It is one of three major resort areas along with Montego Bay on the northwest coast and Negril on the far western tip of Jamaica.

Visitors flock to Ocho Rios because of its pristine beaches, mountainous shoreline and garden-like scenery. It also has a famous natural attraction.

Quick Tips

- Dunn's River Falls is the most popular attraction and one of the best in the Caribbean.
- Ocho Rios Bay Beach is within walking distance of the cruise docks.
- Island Village by the docks is a large shopping, dining and entertainment development.

Attractions and Shore Excursions

Ocho Rios is a popular port of call for cruise ships in part because of its famous and probably most popular attraction – Dunn's River Falls.

It is one of the most famous natural attractions in the Caribbean. We had a blast when we went there.

Visitors to the falls, which cascade more than 600 feet down hillsides, climb up the rocks and water in the form of a daisy chain. The daisy chain, requiring visitors to hold hands, is a bit awkward but necessary for safety on the slippery rocks. Photo opportunities are abundant.

Cruise ships and local excursion companies transport thousands of visitors to the falls every year. The falls are less than a 10-minute drive from Ocho Rios.

Despite the fame of Dunn's River Falls, Dolphin Cove claims to be the No. 1 tourist attraction in Jamaica with locations in Ocho Rios, Negril and Montego Bay.

The Ocho Rios facility is about two miles or three kilometers west of the cruise docks on the way to Dunn's River Falls. The two attractions will fill an entire day for cruise visitors with a large budget.

The beachfront property has been in business since the 1990s and offers a variety of interactions with dolphins, sharks, stingrays, parrots and pirates along with glass bottom boat excursions.

The Blue Hole, 20 minutes outside of Ocho Rios, is another popular shore excursion. It has cascades and bright blue natural swimming pools. This attraction is often offered in combination with other attractions. Prices usually start at $100 per person with discounts for children.

Mystic Mountain Rainforest Adventures, less than 10 minutes from the docks, has chairlifts, a bobsled ride and zip lines among other activities. Prices vary according to each offer with some costing less than $50 and others costing more than $150 per person.

Other area attractions include river rafting and canoeing on the nearby White River or hiking or cycling in the Blue Mountains, but they are more appropriate for stayover visitors and not cruise visitors.

In addition, many visitors go to Eden Falls, Fern Gully and Shaw Park Botanical Gardens. Excursion companies offer jeep safaris, ATV safaris, zip line canopy tours and a bamboo rafting trip, among other adventures.

Ocho Rios has two 18-hole golf courses at the Sandals Resort in Upton about five miles or nine kilometers southeast of Ocho Rios and the Jewel Runaway Bay course about 16 miles or 26 kilometers east of the cruise terminal at Runaway Bay.

Nearby Beaches

Cruise visitors who would rather spend time on the beach can either walk to one near the docks or spend money on a taxi, rental car or excursion bus to get to more.

They will find an easy and convenient choice at Ocho Rios Bay Beach right by the cruise docks. It is a 10-minute walk to the east of the port. Just look to the left on arriving at the docks.

One of the best beaches in the area is the quarter-mile-long Reggae Beach, which is about four miles or seven kilometers east of the cruise terminal. It is known for its beauty, serenity and snorkeling.

The smaller Mahogany Beach is about one and a half miles east of the port. It's a less appealing option than the others, but it is convenient for anyone walking in that direction through the town.

Bamboo Beach, formerly known as Reggae Beach, is a larger and better option about five miles to the east of the port. It is included in some cruise line shore excursions.

Another shore excursion option combines Pearly Beach with the nearby Dunn's River Falls. They are just three miles west of the port.

The more secluded James Bond Beach for fans of the early movies in the series is the farthest of the bunch. It is 13 miles or 30 minutes each of the port.

Shopping / Restaurants

The closest shopping is Island Village right by the cruise docks. It is a large shopping, dining and entertainment development. It has an outdoor concert venue, reggae and Jamaican art museums, a casino, water sports and of course plenty of shopping.

Like every other major port in the Caribbean, Ocho Rios has a market of local arts and crafts. The Ocho Rios Craft Park, located by Main Street, has 150 shopping stalls with the usual array of handmade and commercial souvenirs for sale.

A third shopping complex, Island Plaza, is located in the center of Ocho Rios It also has a wide range of commercial and handmade arts, crafts and souvenirs.

Note that all merchandise on sales has a 16.5 percent consumer tax. Also be prepared to negotiate with the vendors over price.

Getting Around / Transportation

Taxis and excursion buses are the best option for getting around Ocho Rios and visiting major attractions such as Dunn's River Falls. The area has a few local and national car rental companies that serve cruise visitors. Public buses are not recommended.

Weather / Best Time to Go

Jamaica is one of the warmest islands in the Caribbean and popular with western Caribbean cruises from December through March.

Average high temperatures range from the mid-80s Fahrenheit during the winter to more than 90 in the summer.

Rainfall averages less than one inch from January through March, picks up slightly in April and spikes during a brief rainy season in May and June.

Rain drops off in July and starts to climb again in August as the Caribbean hurricane season starts to become more active.

Total rainfall reaches nearly six inches in September and more than seven inches in October.

Although it's possible to visit Ocho Rios by cruise during the fall, anyone with flexible travel schedules should consider going in the spring instead for lower risk of rain.

Key West: Florida

Western Caribbean

The Key West cruise port in Florida is closer to Cuba than Miami. Visitors will experience a unique blend of cultures, attractions and lifestyles.

This remote island at the southernmost tip of the United States is growing in popularity as a cruise port because of expanded port facilities as well as the island's history and attractions.

Even though it isn't in the Caribbean, it is a fairly common stop on western Caribbean cruises, especially ones that embark from Tampa and other Florida ports.

Visitors will disembark at Pier B, Navy Mole or the Mallory Square Dock next to Mallory Square Plaza. All of them are located on the west side of the island where they will find the historical Old Town and spend most of their time.

Quick Tips

- The highly commercial town center is the main attraction.
- Free shuttles take cruise visitors around the city.

- April and May are the best months to visit.

Attractions and Shore Excursions

Free shuttles take cruise passengers from the docks to the town center where they will find plenty of shopping, dining and other things to do. The town center is one big open-air shopping mall.

Free shuttles carry visitors around town.

Visitors who are willing to walk a bit will find the former homes of such famous people as Ernest Hemingway, Tennessee Williams, Elizabeth Bishop, Robert Frost and Jimmy Buffett.

One of the closest is the Harry S. Truman Little White House at 111 Front Street. It served as a getaway for Truman during his Presidency as well as Dwight Eisenhower and John F. Kennedy.

The Ernest Hemingway Home and Museum at 907 Whitehead Street is less than one mile from each of the cruise docks.

Mallory Square is a plaza with nightly entertainment and sunset watching. The amount of entertainment varies with each night. It is next to the Key West Aquarium and Duval Street, which is the main tourist drag.

Fort Zachary Taylor protected the Florida Keys during the Civil War. This state historical park also has a beach, fishing, snorkeling and picnic grounds. It is about one mile from Mallory Square on the southwest tip of the island.

The Florida Keys Eco Discovery Center, 35 East Quay Road, has more than 6,000 square feet of exhibits educating visitors about the Florida Keys National Marine Sanctuary.

The sanctuary is one of 14 marine protected areas that make up the National Marine Sanctuary System. Exhibits include a mock-up of Aquarius, the only underwater ocean laboratory in the world. Entrance is free.

Dry Tortugas National Park lies about 68 miles west of Key West in the Gulf of Mexico. The park consists of about 100 square miles, mostly open water and seven small islands that are the most isolated keys of the Florida Keys.

They are accessible only by chartered boat or seaplane from Key West. The park is mostly known for the six-sided Fort Jefferson.

The Conch Tourist Train is a trolley that drives along Duval Street and makes various stops including Old Town, the waterfront and the Hemingway house. The "train" and Old Town Trolley are the two main motorized tour services on key west. $$

The Mel Fisher Maritime Museum, 200 Greene Street or a few blocks south of Mallory Square, has many shipwreck displays including a 77.76 carat emerald and other valuable items from a 1622 fleet of Spanish treasure galleons. It also has educational exhibits and laboratory tours. The museum claims it is the only fully accredited museum in the Florida Keys. $$

Audubon House and Tropical Gardens, 205 Whitehead Street, is the restored mansion of the Geiger family, which lived there for 110 years. The Museum commemorates the 1832 visit to Key West of artist John James Audubon and displays his artwork throughout the mansion. The gardens often have more than 200 orchids in bloom along with a koi pond and herb garden.

Weather / Best Time to Go

The average high temperature in Key West ranges from the mid 70s Fahrenheit in January to the high 80s Fahrenheit in the summer, according to the U.S. National Weather Service.

The island has a dry season from November through May when the average rainfall is two to three inches a month. The rainy season peaks in September with an average rainfall of nearly seven inches.

The best time to go for a combination of warm temperatures and low risk of rain is April or May.

Labadee: Haiti

Eastern Caribbean

Few tourist opportunities exist in Haiti because of the country's political and economic instability. The private cruise port of Labadee is an exception.

Labadee, owned by Royal Caribbean, is on the north coast of Haiti in a remote area of the country. It has a beautiful white beach surrounded by lush mountains, an aqua park for children, parasailing, kayaking, banana boat and shopping in a local village, among other activities.

Celebrity and Azamara cruise lines visit Labadee in addition to Royal Caribbean.

Labadee is a stop on some western Caribbean cruises. Visitors will see lagoon-like bays surrounded by forest-covered mountains. The homes of locals who provide workers for the facility as well as sell arts and crafts often peek out from the mountain sides.

Quick Tips

- Labadee is best known for beaches.
- It has the longest zip line in the world over water.
- Shopping is mostly limited to local arts and crafts.

Attractions and Shore Excursions

The shallow bays offer excellent snorkeling for families as well as some energetic banana boat rides.

Labadee continues to grow and has added several major features in recent years. Some are available without charge and some require an extra fee.

The Dragon's Breath Flight Line is the longest flight line in the world over water. It allows visitors to go 500 feet up the mountain and zip down on a cable more than 2,600 feet to the beach below at 40-50 miles an hour.

Dragon's Splash Waterslide goes 300 feet through 10 turns and takes people into a splash zone. Dragon's Tail Coaster goes 30 miles an hour and offers views of the surrounding area. Arawak Aqua Park has trampolines, water slides, a rolling log and other water toys.

Labadee also has kayaking, parasailing and jet skis available for rent.

Dining is available on the beach at three different cafes. Visitors who rent a cabana get meals from the cafes included in the price.

Nearby Beaches

Labadee is perhaps best known for the quality of its beaches. They have some of the whitest and finest sand in the Caribbean.

Dragon Tail Beach on the north shore of the peninsula is the largest one. It is good for swimming, snorkeling and resting.

Barefoot Beach Club is where visitors go who are renting cabanas. Nellie's Beach is another option for anyone renting a cabana.

Columbus Cove is the place for water toys such as Arawak Aqua Park and Dragon's Splash Waterslide. Adrenaline Beach is farthest from the ship and the best option for sunbathing and small crowds.

Shopping

Local residents who sell arts and crafts in Haiti and Dominican Republic are among the most aggressive people we have met in the Caribbean. This includes our visit to Labadee.

Be polite but firm and assertive when saying no. Keep in mind that they freely negotiate prices, so hagglers will find plenty of chances to bring down prices.

Examine any wood products for purchase with care. We brought home a beautiful mask, only to find that it had termites.

Weather / Best Time to Go

Temperatures in Labadee average in the mid to upper 80s Fahrenheit or about 30 degrees Celsius during most of the year.

Like the rest of the western Caribbean, Haiti has a dry season from December until March. This is the most popular time to visit.

Martinique: Fort-de-France

Eastern Caribbean

Martinique may be the most French of the four French islands in the Caribbean.

English is not spoken nearly as much by the locals as elsewhere. Many of the signs are in French rather than English.

As such, the island draws more tourists from France than English-speaking countries. But that doesn't stop cruise ships with English speakers from stopping there.

Many ships dock at the Tourelles Terminal, which is near the edge of Fort-de-France, the capital of the island. The cruise docks are located on the southwestern edge of the island.

Visitors won't find much at the cruise terminal. Instead, the heart of the visit lies at Fort-de-France, which is a five-minute taxi ride or 15-minute walk to the center of town.

Other cruise ships dock right at the center of town at the growing Port Simone Terminal, which gives visitors easy access to everything. From here, it is a quick jaunt.

The unique architecture of Schoelcher library is popular with photographers.

Quick Tips

- Use the Visitor Information Center at the Pointe Simon docks as a starting point.
- Fort Saint Louis, La Savane Park and Schoelcher library are popular attractions in the city.
- Outside of the city, Mount Pelée is a renowned dormant volcano,

hiking attraction and highest peak on the island.

Arrival Tips

Like other Caribbean islands, Martinique is expanding its efforts to appeal to cruise ship passengers.

The Martinique Cruise Village at Pointe Simon is a small facility of vendors and information booths with multilingual speakers. It is at open during the peak cruise season until mid April.

Inside Fort-de-France are city stewards in red jackets who also are multilingual and give directions and answer questions, according to the Martinique Tourism Authority. (For the record, we didn't see any, but that doesn't mean they aren't around.)

Vendors include local clothing, jewelry and accessory designers, locally produced skin care products and perfumes, souvenir shops, local artists exhibiting their paintings and tasty snacks. All vendors accept payment in US Dollars.

The experience is enhanced with live local music, entertainment, rum tasting, and greetings by multilingual hostesses.

Attractions and Shore Excursions

Fort-de-France is a quite walkable town with cafes, shops and various historical attractions.

Cruise ships and excursion operators offer walking tours of the city for about $40 to $50. Tour guides offer historical and cultural perspectives. But independent visitors can easily walk the city on their own.

The 17th century Fort Saint Louis is a massive fort on a rocky peninsula just to the east of the city.

Cruise visitors who disembark at Pointe Simon can walk off the docks and go several hundred yards to the right to reach the fort.

It is still active as a naval base. Visitors can tour the fort but not the base.

La Savane, just to the left of the fort, is a spare 12-acre park with a headless, vandalized statue of Napoleon's wife, Empress Josephine. Splatters of red paint add a macabre touch to the decapitated statue.

Right next to La Savane is Schoelcher library, one of the most photographed attractions on the island because of its beautiful architecture.

Mount Pelée is a renowned volcano and the highest peak on the island at 4,500 feet. The site is a National Biological Reserve with views of both the Atlantic ocean and the Caribbean sea on clear days. A summit trail is available for experienced hikers. The volcano is located about one hour and 15 minutes northwest of Fort-de-France via excursion bus.

The island has one 71-par golf course at the Martinique Golf and Country Club at Les Trois Ilets. It offers 18 holes totaling 6,640 yards. It also has a driving range and putting green. The course is a 30-minute drive south of Fort-de-France.

Garden of Balata is a 15-minute drive north of the city. It is a private botanical garden with 3,000 tropical species open to the public for a fee.

Nearby Beaches

Martinique isn't one of the better beach destinations for cruises because so few beaches are near the Fort-de-France cruise port.

Some of the best beaches such as Grande Anse des Salines lie an hour or more away from Fort-de-France. But few excursion companies and cruise lines offer trips to Grand Anse because of its distance.

Pointe du Bout is 30 minutes south of the city, and Anse DuFour is 45 minutes away. So cruise visitors who really want to visit a beach may have to rent a car or taxi.

If taking an excursion trip, be sure to find out the amount of travel time versus the amount of time on the beach. Some trips require more travel time than actual time at the location.

Shopping / Restaurants

Fort-de-France is less developed commercially for tourists than other cruise ports. It doesn't have the same high level of ship visits such as Nassau, Grand Cayman, St. Maarten, St. Thomas and others.

What counts as the main drag is Avenue Loulou Beulaville, which is the first street running parallel to the water and in front of the Point Simone terminal.

Shops and restaurants are scattered haphazardly beyond the Tourist Information Center at Point Simone. From the center, take either Rue du Commerce or Rue Francois Arago away from the docks. Before leaving, check the center for tips on the best restaurants.

The covered marketplace in the heart of downtown Fort-de-France is a truly local shopping experience with vendors selling everything from local foods to handmade straw products.

Getting Around / Transportation

Fort-de-France is one of the better walking around ports because most everything worth seeing is reachable on foot from the Pointe Simon cruise docks. Passengers who disembark at Tourelles Terminal will need a taxi to reach the city center.

Buses travel between Fort-de-France and popular tourist attractions, but they have a reputation for being unpredictable. Look for signs on buses that say "TC" (for Taxi Collectifs).

Otherwise, passengers wanting to go outside of the Fort-de-France city center will need a taxi, rental car or excursion bus.

Weather / Best Times to Go

The average daily high temperatures range from the low 80s Fahrenheit during the winter to the high 80s in the summer. Nighttime temperatures range in the low to mid 70s.

Martinique is a lush island thanks to a high amount of rain throughout the year. It is one of the rainiest islands in the Caribbean.

The island historically has averaged three to four inches a rain per month during the best times to visit -- February through April. Rainfall starts to climb in May and reaches a high point of as much as 10 inches a month from August through November.

Panama: Colón

Western Caribbean

The Colón cruise port is the gateway to the Panama Canal on the Caribbean side and one of the more popular stops on western Caribbean cruises.

That fact might lead someone to think that the main attraction is the Panama Canal and the famous locks that raise and low ships as they cross between the Atlantic and Pacific oceans.

They would be right, but Colón has more to offer. Cruise visitors usually arrive at Colón 2000 or Pier 6 of Cristóbal port on the south side of Limon Bay. The location on the bay is important to know for the sake of seeing as much as possible in the shortest amount of time.

Colón is the provincial capital and the province has Central America's largest port system.

The area around the Colón 2000 terminal is known for its restaurants and shopping, while the area around the nearby Cristóbal port is known for its craft markets.

The two locations are about three miles apart and take 10 minutes to reach by regulated taxis.

Colón has a reputation for street crime, but government authorities have made a strong effort to make tourists feel secure within the duty-free zone. Make sure to use a registered taxi when traveling outside of the zone and don't displays wallets or jewelry.

While the duty free zone is packed with shopping, the biggest draws for anyone visiting Colón are the shore excursions.

Quick Tips

- Lake Gatún and Panama Canal tours are the dominant attractions.
- Beach lovers will have to drive long distances to find good ones.
- Colón Free Zone, which is the largest duty-free zone in the western hemisphere and the second largest in the world.

Attractions and Shore Excursions

For first-time visitors, it is useful to know that the Panama Canal was made possible not only because of the narrow width of Panama between the Atlantic and Pacific oceans and a huge investment of money and labor (as well as lives). It also was made possible by the presence of the sprawling Lake Gatún.

Limon Bay connects with Lake Gatún at the Gatún Locks, the first of the famous locks on the Atlantic side that raise and lower ships going through Panama and that need to adjust to different terrains and sea levels.

The lake and the locks are only about a 25 minute drive from Colón via taxi or excursion bus.

A tour of the locks is not the most exciting experience for a cruise traveler in the Caribbean, but it is one of the most impressive and educational excursions. The tour is highly recommended for families in particular.

Anyone on a tight schedule can visit the locks and return to Colón within a few hours. Other visitors usually combine the locks with other activities including a kayak or canoe tour around Lake Gatún to view the numerous species of wildlife that lives there or boat tours for the less active.

Two of the next best attractions in the area are in opposite directions of each other along the Atlantic coast.

Fort San Lorenzo, one of the oldest Spanish forts in America, lies about 45 minutes west of Colón. Built in 1597, this UNESCO World Heritage Site was designed to protect the mouth of Chagres River.

The Chagres was an entry point for boats that traveled upstream to reach Venta de Cruces. From that point, they walked to Panama City on a trail Camino de Cruces.

Portobelo National Park is another UNESCO World Heritage site located about an hour east of Colón. Christopher Columbus discovered and named the landing site Portobelo, which is Italian for "beautiful port," in 1502.

Francisco Valverde y Mercado founded the city of San Felipe de Portobelo in 1597. The Spaniards shipped gold and silver from Peru, unloaded it at Panama City and carried it on mules across the isthmus to Portobelo. Visitors can see the remains of the original fortifications that protected the plunder from pirates.

Nearby Beaches

Colón is known for the above shore excursions, but it's not known as a beach destination.

Although Panama has its share of good beaches, most of them are located elsewhere, like Bocas del Toro.

Cruise visitors to Colón with a passion for beaches can go to Playa La Angosta, which is about a 40 minute drive from Colón, or to Isla Grande, an island about an hour's drive away.

Shopping / Restaurants

Visitors can start their shopping at the modest Colón 2000 Mall right by the cruise docks. It is known for a handful of shops, a casino and a safe environment.

Colón claims the second largest duty-free shopping zone in the world. The much bigger opportunity lies at the Colón Free Zone southeast of the cruise docks. It has more than 3,000 companies represented on more than 1,000 acres of land.

Cristobal Pier on the eastern side of the Panama Canal has an active crafts market.

Perhaps a better option is for passengers to hop on a train and go to Panama City. The distance is 46 miles, and the ride lasts about an hour. Passengers can board the train at the Atlantic Passenger Station in Mount Hope near the Port of Cristobal. It is a mile and a half southwest of the cruise terminal. Multiple cruise lines offer this trip as an excursion.

Getting Around / Transportation

Colón is better known as a port where cruise passengers take excursions into the countryside or over to Panama City rather than staying in the city. Although taxi service is available in Colón, there are few options for traveling short distances.

"Rather than spending the day in Colon, many cruise passengers choose instead to participate in shore excursions arranged by their ships or tours organized independently," as one cruise line said.

Weather / Best Times to Go

Panama weather on the Caribbean coast enjoys drier weather from late winter to early summer and wetter weather from early summer to late fall.

The wet weather in the second half of the year is the result of the Caribbean hurricane season. It brings heavier rains to the Caribbean and parts of Central America. Panama rarely gets hit by a hurricane, but instead has spikes in rain.

Temperatures are warm throughout the year with average highs nearing 90 degrees Fahrenheit or 32 Celsius.

Progreso: Yucatan Mexico

Western Caribbean

The Mexican cruise port at Progreso is an up-and-coming destination on the northern coast of the Yucatán Peninsula.

It is a regular port of call on western Caribbean cruises from Gulf Coast ports in the United States. Short-term cruises often include Progreso and Cozumel, while longer cruises will go to Cozumel, Belize and Roatan.

The Terminal Remota, Progreso's most unique attraction, is a four-mile-long dock. It receives nearly 100 cruise ships and more than 300,000 passengers every year. Passengers take a bus from the ship to the city.

Quick Tips

- Progreso Beach and the Malecon boardwalk are top local attractions.

- Chichen Itza is the best and farthest major attraction.
- December through February are the best times to go.

Chichen Itza is a major attraction for Progreso cruise visitors.

Where is Progreso Yucatán?

Progreso is 200 miles west of Cancun on the northern coast of the Yucatán Peninsula. It faces the Gulf of Mexico rather than the Caribbean Sea. The port is 100 miles northwest of Chichen Itza, one of the most famous Mayan ruins in the world.

Like Cancun, Progreso is on a narrow cape of land that extends out from the coast. The water surrounding the cape is shallow, so cruise visitors will disembark at one of the longest piers in the world.

Because of its location, it is more likely a port of call for cruises that begin in Gulf of Mexico ports such as Galveston and New Orleans instead of cruises that begin in Florida.

Attractions and Shore Excursions

Nearby attractions are mostly limited to Progreso beach with its mile-long promenade known as Malecon. It offers souvenir shops, cafes, a nearby marketplace featuring local arts and crafts, and a 120-foot lighthouse built in the late 1800s.

Otherwise, most of the activities with the Progreso area involve cruise ship excursions. Better-known attractions lie elsewhere.

The most famous and popular attraction is the Mayan ruins at Chichen Itza, which is located about halfway between Progreso and Cancun. The ruins are about 98 miles or a nearly two-hour drive from the port.

But the drive is worth it. This ancient city, which was first built around 900 A.D., is a UNESCO World Heritage site and the second most-visited archaeological site in Mexico. The massive ruins are both educational and astonishing for their size.

Smaller Mayan ruins are located at Uxmal, Mayapan and especially Dzibilchaltun, which is only 12 miles from the port.

Dzibilchaltun, whose name means "place of the stone writing," was an ancient Mayan ceremonial and administrative center, the Mexico Tourism Board says. Temple of the Seven Dolls is one of the noteworthy structures because of the dolls discovered there.

The site has a museum with displays of Mayan culture and artifacts discovered at Dzibilchaltun. Some of the artifacts were found at the bottom of the 120-foot-deep Xlacah cenote, a freshwater pool that was created by an underground river.

Prices for these Mayan excursions are often less than $100 per person with discounts for children.

Other Attractions

Another option outside of Progreso is the city of Merida, which is a 40-minute or 24-mile bus ride from the port to the city's center. The much larger city of Merida offers more shopping and restaurants in addition to museums, plazas and historic buildings.

Many of the buildings in the historic center of Merida, including those on and around the Plaza Grande (central plaza), were built during the colonial period through the 18th and 19th centuries.

One of the top Merida attractions is the Cathedral de San Ildefonso. It is the oldest cathedral on the North America continent. The cathedral was built in the late 1500s using stones from ruined Mayan pyramids and temples, the Mexico Tourism Board says.

Nearby Beaches

Progreso Beach is the quick and easy option for most cruise visitors because it is by the dock.

Otherwise, few beach excursions are available because Progreso Beach / Malecon is so easily accessible. Some cruise lines do offer access to private beach clubs such as Kokomo Beach Club at between $50 and $100 per person depending on the amenities.

Weather / Best Times to Go

Like most destinations on Mexico's Caribbean and Gulf of Mexico coasts,

Progreso has a distinct dry period and a distinct wet period because of the Caribbean hurricane season.

Even though the hurricane season runs from June through November, Progreso's dry season begins in November with about 2.5 inches of rain historically, according to averages from the Mexico Ministry of Tourism.

The dry season brings about one inch of rain each month from December through April and increases to about three inches in May. It starts climbing until it reaches a high point of about seven inches in September.

Temperatures are hot throughout the year with the average highs ranging from 88 degrees Fahrenheit or 31 degrees Celsius in December and January to 97 Fahrenheit or 36 Celsius in May. High temperatures in the summer make the winter a better time to cruise to Progreso.

The best time to go is December through February for comfortable temperatures and low risk of rain.

Roatan: Coxen Hole

Western Caribbean

Roatan gets plenty of attention on travel and real estate cable channels in part because it is such an inviting island.

It is inviting because of long white sand beaches and great snorkeling and diving spots. It also is a convenient cruise destination.

The largest of the Bay Islands off the coast of Honduras is small in size but growing in popularity with western Caribbean cruises.

Its location only 137 miles southwest of Belize City makes it an easy island to reach. Its small size makes the visit a quick one too.

Most Roatan cruise port visitors will arrive at Coxen Hole. It is capital of the Bay Island and the largest city with a population of about 5,000 people.

Anyone traveling with Carnival will land at the Mahogany Bay cruise port, a Carnival-built complex on 20 acres to the west of Coxen Hole.

It opened in 2009 as part of a trend among cruise lines to build private, commerce-oriented docking facilities.

Both docks are located on the southwestern side of the island.

Quick Tips

- Coxen Hole and Mahogany Bay are the main cruise ports.
- West End Beach and West End Village are among the most popular attractions.
- The island is well-known for snorkeling and diving among its famous coral reefs.

Attractions and Shore Excursions

Coxen Hole is the island capital, largest town and the main cruise port. With a population of about 5,000 people, it has a smaller number of restaurants and duty-free shops for visitors compared to larger ports in the Caribbean.

Roatan Marine Park is a protected area of western Roatan between West Bay and Sandy Bay. It has many of the most popular diving and snorkeling spots and also some of the most popular beaches.

Gumbalimba Park is an animal preserve with parrots, monkeys, iguanas and turkeys, among other creatures. It also botanical gardens, a beach for swimming and other recreational activities. Activities include kayaking, snuba and scuba diving, a zipline canopy tour and the Jolly Roger Sail.

Carambola Botanical Gardens and Trails is across the road from Anthony's Key Resort on the north side of Roatan. It has 40 acres of land for hiking, wildlife viewing and scenic tours. Garden hours are 8 a.m. to 5 p.m.

The Roatan Institute of Marine Science at Anthony's Key Resort is a marine research and educational facility. Visitors can swim, snorkel or dive with dolphins.

Because local residents eat iguanas, conservationists have created The Iguana Farm to protect and breed the dwindling population. The farm has several hundred iguanas. The best time to see them is early afternoon at feeding time. The farm is in French Key, just past French Harbour.

Visitors can dive as much as 2,000 feet on the Idabel, which is called the world's deepest passenger submarine, and view marine life through a Plexiglas bubble. The tour is chartered and can carry two passengers and a pilot at any one time.

The Butterfly Garden is a five-minute walk from the main entrance of West End Village. Other than butterflies, the garden has tropical plants and trees, many hummingbirds, and a small collection of parrots, macaws, and toucans that have been acquired as rescue birds.

Nearby Beaches

Anyone not interested in snorkeling or diving may want to spend the day at the island's famous beaches.

West Bay Beach on the southwestern tip of the island is the most famous and most popular because of its extensive white sands, resorts, restaurants and other facilities. Most cruise excursions go to a section called Tabyana Beach.

It is about a 30-minute drive from Coxen Hole and 45 minutes from Mahogany Bay, so cruise visitors need a taxi, bus, rental car or excursion bus to get there.

Water taxis connect West End Beach with West End Village, which has an active nightlife, for about $2.60 U.S. at the time of this writing. It also is about 10 minutes by car.

Half Moon Bay is another popular beach. It's a 20-minute drive from the cruise port.

Shopping / Restaurants

Roatan does not receive as many western Caribbean cruise visitors as Grand Cayman or Cozumel. As a result, the shopping opportunities are more limited.

Coxen Hole has an open air market, shopping plaza and supermarkets. West Bay Beach has stalls featuring local artists and retailers.

Roatan has more than 100 restaurants. They are concentrated around Coxen Hole, Mahogany Bay, West End Village, West End Beach and other popular tourist areas.

Restaurants around Coxen Hole include Frenchy's 44, Bojangles, Haydee's Diner, Nardo's Bar and Grill, and Wood's Place.

Local cuisine includes baleadas, pastilles, conch and other seafood specialities. Other local favorites include Honduran coffee, fresh local fruit smoothies and local gelato flavours.

Getting Around / Transportation

Roatan is only about 2.5 miles wide at its widest point but 40 miles long, so adventurous people with plenty of time will want to take advantage of available transportation options.

Many of the car rental agencies are located at the airport. None are located at the docks at the time of this writing, but many of them do provide pickup at both docks.

Taxi rates are fairly low. The rate from Coxen Hole to West End is about $2.20 U.S., according to Tourism Roatan. The rate from Coxen Hole to West End Beach is about $7.10.

It is important to note that the rates are not fixed by a government agency or taxi association, so ask for the rates before getting into the taxi. Taxis sitting right by the docks are more likely to charge higher rates.

Two bus routes begin in Coxen Hole and go to the various popular points on the island including West End Bay. They cost about $2.60 one way to West End and Sandy Bay for a 10-minute ride.

Weather / Best Times to Go

The official dry season in Roatan runs from April through late July with an average high temperature of 86 degrees Fahrenheit and 30 degrees Celsius.

A rainy season tends to hit the island from late July to early September The peak rainy season goes from mid-January to the end of February.

As a result, western Caribbean cruises that visit the island are often quite popular during the spring and early summer.

Roatan: Mahogany Bay

Western Caribbean

The Mahogany Bay cruise port on the island of Roatan is another example of the growing number of private cruise ports in the Caribbean.

Mahogany Bay has a private beach right by the docks.

Roatan, one of the Bay islands off the coast of Honduras, has attracted a growing number of cruise visits to its capital and major port at the city of Coxen Hole.

But Carnival Cruise Lines opted to build a cruise center at Dixon Cove, which lies about 20 minutes east of Coxen Hole. It draws Carnival cruise brands including the flagship Carnival name, Princess and Holland America.

The port can accommodate two ships with up to 8,000 passengers. The Mahogany Bay experience depends quite a bit on how many ships and passengers are there that day.

Quick Tips

- Mahogany Beach is an eight-minute walk from the docks.
- The private port has a half dozen bars and restaurants and a dozen duty-free shops.
- April and May are the best months to visit for warm temperatures and low risk of rain.

Attractions and Shore Excursions

On arrival, cruise passengers will easily see the port's three main attractions from the decks of their ships. They are the cruise center, the beach and both the bridge and the "Magical Flying Chair" that connect the cruise center with the beach.

Cruise passengers on board their ships also will see a partially sunken ship in the harbor.

Duty-free shopping is impossible to avoid at Mahogany Bay. Cruise passengers must pass through the Dufry duty-free shop to get to the other attractions. From there, visitors have a moderate uphill walk from the cruise docks to the cruise center.

The cruise center is a 20-acre, open-air complex with a variety of shops and restaurants. We found the prices, products and services mostly in line with other cruise ports.

As beach lovers, we especially liked Mahogany Beach. It's a 10-acre private island with an 825-foot-long beach with an open-air restaurant, beach volleyball court and many water sports activities.

Visitors have another brief but flat walk from the cruise center to the beach. Although the beach has hundreds of free chaise lounges, cruise passengers should arrive early on days when two ships are docked. Only a handful sit under shade trees.

Some people may want to skip the cruise center and go straight from the ship to the beach. A cruise employee said the beach is an eight-minute walk from the docks. I found he was right for people who walk at a moderate pace.

Anyone who doesn't want to walk from the cruise center to the beach can take a chair lift. The lift is $14 for teens and adults, $8 for children 4 to 12 and free for children under 4. The prices serve as an all-day pass. Prices are subject to change.

Shopping / Restaurants

An arts and crafts market has more than a dozen vendors. Jewelers include Diamonds International and Tanzanite International. Other brands include Pirana Joe and Del Sol.

The port has a half dozen themed bars and restaurants. The open-air Fat Tuesday's bar on top of Monkey Hill has views of the ships and the gardens. Crazy Ice Gelateria has a variety of ice creams, while Espresso Americano specializes in coffees and espressos using Honduran beans.

Hurricane Hole's focus is specialty cocktails, and Playa Tortugas Chill 'n' Grill serves bar cuisine. Fish lovers can go to Hideaway Fishery for the fresh catch of the day.

Transportation

Visitors who want to leave the confines of the cruise port will mainly have to rely on taxis or excursion buses. One car rental agency serves the port.

A taxi manager told us it would cost $20 for one to four people to go one way to Coxen Hole for more shopping, dining and sightseeing. The city is less than 20 minutes away.

The Mahogany Bay Taxi Association has divided the island into a series of zones with different rates for each zone. The trip to Coxen Hole was $20 per taxi, while all other zones range from $10 to $25 per person.

Weather

Like Coxen Hole, Mahogany Bay weather has average daytime temperatures ranging from the low 80s Fahrenheit in the winter to 90 degrees in the summer.

The rainiest months are October, November and December while the driest months are April and May, according to the Roatan Tourism Bureau.

During our recent visit in April, the temperature was in the high 80s Fahrenheit. The sky did not have a single cloud.

San Juan: Puerto Rico

Eastern and Southern Caribbean

San Juan is a major cruise port for trips to the southern and western Caribbean. The city's great history is unique.

Many attractions, vibrant shopping and the same white beaches and aqua water makes it attractive as a destination on its own. Our time in San Juan was as pleasant as any other we have experienced.

Although Spanish is the preferred language, English was spoken by about 90 percent of the people with whom we had contact.

The cruise port is an easy one to visit and especially to tour because of the language, culture, economy and size.

Quick Tips

- January through March are the most popular months for cruise visits.
- English is widely spoken, but do expect to meet some people who don't speak English.
- Old San Juan is the most popular attraction and near the cruise terminals.

Attractions and Shore Excursions

Touring Old San Juan is a easy choice for most people starting and ending their Caribbean cruise out of San Juan.

It is the most popular tourist attraction in the port and easy to access from the main cruise docks. In fact, moderately fit people can walk from the docks to this historical dining, shopping and entertainment enclave.

The impressive forts of San Cristobal and El Morro will please history buffs. Shoppers will enjoy cobblestone streets, numerous shops and the relaxing plazas.

Anyone who simply wants a casual stroll will love walking along the outer wall of La Muralla with tall trees, sculptures, water fountains and especially the lovely sunset.

Another highlight is the Cathedral of San Juan Bautista. It is the second oldest cathedral in the Americas and one of the oldest buildings in Old San Juan.

La Fortaleza in Old San Juan is the official residence of the Puerto Rico governor. It was built in the mid 1500s to protect the San Juan harbor. This UNESCO World Heritage Site is the oldest executive mansion in continuous use in the New World.

Cruise ships often offer a guided tour of Old San Juan for a fee that may cost around $100 per adult.
Visitors with an interest in art may want to see the Museum of Art of Puerto Rico.

The museum's collection has works dating from the 17th century to the present. They are displayed in 24 galleries.
It is four miles southeast of the cruise docks at 299 Ave De Diego.

Cruise excursions include a few unusual trips outside of San Juan. The Bacardi Rum Distillery, the largest in the world, is a 15-minute drive from San Juan. The distillery is one of the most popular tourist attractions in Puerto Rico.

Visitors can see vast fermentation vats, high-speed bottling machinery and the Bacardi family museum. They also can sample the famous rum and buy souvenirs or Bacardi products at the gift shop.

Cruise ships also offer a tour of the distillery and include other sites as well. Expect to pay $50 to $100 per person depending on the amenities.

Nearby Beaches

San Juan has several major beaches for cruise visitors.

The most recommended is Escambron beach in Puerta de Tierra. The beach has snorkeling, biking, picnicking facilities and views of both districts.

It is a little more than one mile east of the cruise docks at the Luis Munoz Rivera Park between Old San Juan and the Condado district. Cruisers will need a taxi to get there.

Balneario of Carolina is about seven miles east of the cruise docks. Another option is Balneario Punta Salinas in Toa Baja, about seven to eight miles west of the docks.

Shopping / Restaurants

Old San Juan isn't just one of the largest and most popular historical attractions in the entire Caribbean. It's also one of the largest shopping and dining districts as well.

Shoppers can easily take several hours to explore all of the options.

Cruise visitors will find plenty of shops and restaurants to suit just about any interest. But don't be surprised to see many of the same kinds of goods that shops in other cruise ports have to offer.

Getting Around / Transportation

The San Juan cruise port has docks in two locations.

The Old San Juan piers are on the coast right by Old San Juan, which makes it easy for passengers to walk to the historic area.

The Pan American Pier is on the other side of the harbor, which means most passengers will have to take a taxi to get to the city. The distance is nearly three miles and takes about 10 minutes to get there in normal traffic.

Taxi rates are standard. But it's always a good idea to ask for rates before getting into any taxi.

The public bus system routes include the Old San Juan pier. We found it was much less expensive than a taxi but took a lot more time. It's a decent option for budget travelers who have extra time in San Juan.

Weather / Best Times to Go

San Juan's average weather is similar to most other Caribbean islands with one exception: it doesn't rain as much during the peak times of the hurricane season.

The Caribbean hurricane season officially runs from June 1 through Nov. 30 each year. The highest amount of rainfall usually hits in September and October with some destinations experiencing as much as 10 to 15 inches of rain in September.

San Juan's historical average is about five to six inches each from August through November, which is still enough to discourage cruise visits. The number of days that it rains averages about 14 from July through December.

San Juan temperatures are more predictable with average highs ranging from the low 80s Fahrenheit during the winter to the high 80s during the summer. Average lows range from the low 70s to high 70s, mainly at night.

March is the most popular time to visit San Juan. It also will be the most crowded in major tourist attractions like Old San Juan. Prices will likely rise as well.

April will have fewer crowds, warmer temperatures and only slightly more rain. May should be avoided because of the brief rainy season.

Otherwise, the next best months to visit Puerto Rico are June and July when average rainfall is about four inches, temperatures are warm enough for swimming and crowds are usually moderate in size.

Santo Tomás de Castilla: Guatemala

Western Caribbean

Santo Tomás de Castilla is the smallest active cruise port in the western Caribbean region.

This port village in the Izabal Department of Guatemala is much more active as a commercial port along with the nearby and much larger city of Puerto Barrios. Anyone who drives between the two may not tell where one ends and the other begins.

As few as four cruise ships visit Santo Tomás de Castilla in a single month.

The cruise season usually lasts between November and April of each year.

The cruise port has a small but active terminal building.

On arriving, cruise visitors will see a massive shipyard for commercial shipping, a small station for the Guatemala Navy and a welcome center for cruise passengers. Excursion buses, boats and booths are less than a hundred feet from the ship plank.

For some people, such a quiet port may feel like a welcome change from the massive shopping complexes that now fill most cruise ports in the Caribbean. It's an easy port to visit.

Quick Tips

- Shoppers will find goods in only a single long building.
- Popular excursions include nature tours, a Spanish fort and Mayan ruins.

- The best time to go for weather is March and April.

Where is Santo Tomás de Castilla?

Santo Tomás de Castilla lies on the small stretch of Guatemala coast between Belize to the north and Honduras to the south.

The short length of Guatemala's Caribbean coast -- less than 50 miles in a straight line-- is why the port is so important for commercial traffic. There are no other major ports on the Caribbean side of the country.

The port is only 142 miles west of Roatan and 125 miles south of Belize City. Western Caribbean cruises usually visit two out of these three ports because they are so close to each other.

Cruise Terminal

The cruise terminal consists of a large warehouse-like structure just a few hundred feet from the docks.

At the entrance, look straight ahead to see a desk for the Guatemala Tourism Commission. Attendants have maps of the country, answer questions and help with other needs.

A row of food and beverage vendors lies along the left side of the building. A stage sits on the right side. Various bands play throughout the day for the entertainment of passengers. Some of them are quite good.

Local arts and crafts vendors fill most of the remainder of the cruise terminal. Vendors will speak to passengers but not get pushy. Their prices are both reasonable and negotiable.

There are no shops or restaurants elsewhere at the port.

Attractions and Shore Excursions

Despite being a small port, cruise visitors have a variety of options including natural, historical and cultural.

Popular tourist attractions include the Rio Dulce river canyon, the two cities of Puerto Barrios and Livingston, the San Felipe Castle, and the Mayan ruins at Quirigua.

Visitors to the Rio Dulce river canyon can take a boat to the town of Livingston and from there to the canyon. Livingston also has the nearby Mayan ruins of El Nito.

Some excursions offer a tour of Santo Tomás de Castilla and Puerto Barrios that ends at the pretty Amatique Bay Hotel, which is more like a beach resort than a hotel.

San Felipe Fortress on Lake Izabal is a 90-minute drive from the port. The Quirigua Mayan ruins are also a 90-minute drive from the port. They are known for their carvings rather than temples.

Tourists with hefty budgets can take a small plane from the Puerto Barrios Airport to the major Mayan ruins at Tikal.

Getting Around / Transportation

The main options for getting around are excursion buses and boats. Otherwise, visitors should not plan on taxis, rental cars or public transportation.

Weather

Like most Caribbean ports in Central America, Santo Tomás de Castilla has a brief dry season and a longer rainy season.

The dry season is February to early May when rainfall averages about two inches a month. The rainy season is June until January when rainfall can reach more than 10 inches a month.

Daytime temperatures range from the low 80s Fahrenheit or high 20s Celsius in the winter to the highs 80s Fahrenheit or low 30s Celsius in the summer.

The best months to go for weather are March and April when temperatures are warmer and the risk of rain is low.

St. Kitts: Basseterre

Eastern Caribbean

The St. Kitts cruise port is climbing in popularity because of new and improved docks and several noteworthy attractions.

The island is showing up more often as a destination on eastern Caribbean cruises that might include St. Maarten, San Juan and Grand Turk. The most popular months to visit St. Kitts are January and March.

Visitors will disembark at the capital city of Basseterre on the southern coast of the island. They will find the mostly oval-shaped island is easy to tour because of its small size -- 69 square miles.

Quick Tips

- The St. Kitts Scenic Railway is the best known attraction on the island.
- Getting to the best beaches requires a taxi, rental car or excursion bus.
- The new cruise terminal is massive and offers plenty of shopping.

Cruise visitors arrive at the gate of the St. Kitts cruise port mall.

Attractions and Shore Excursions

Unlike many islands, St. Kitts doesn't just have a cruise terminal that consists of a single building. It has an entire cruise mall.

Port Zante is a duty-free shopping district with more than 60 shops selling the usual variety of goods in Caribbean cruise ports. Visitors can spend a couple of hours doing nothing but shopping and dining at outdoor restaurants.

On some days, colorful performers entertain visitors with dance and music. The district also is the starting point for various shore excursions.

People who walk a few hundred yards through the Port Zante district will find the city of Basseterre, beginning with The Circus. It is an octagonal plaza that resembles a small version of London's famous Piccadilly Circus.

Visitors often photograph the Berkeley Memorial Drinking Fountain and Clock. Erected in 1891, it commemorates a 19th-century politician and estate owner.

Every Caribbean destination has beaches, shopping and nightlife, but practically none of them have a train except St. Kitts.

The St. Kitts Scenic Railway is a narrow gauge train that takes visitors on a three-hour, 30-mile circular tour of the island. The tour consists of 18 miles on the train and 12 miles on tour buses.

The train had been used to transport sugarcane from the island plantations to Basseterre from 1912 to 1949. $$

Other popular attractions include climbing the 3,800-foot Mount Liamuiga and a 45-minute ferry ride to nearby Nevis at about $8 a ticket.

Mount Liamuiga, a dormant volcano that is 3,792 feet high, dominates the western half of the island and acts as one of the major attractions.

Adventurous souls can hike to the top of it for expansive views of the island and the sister island of Nevis.

Nevis is known for hiking and other nature-based land activities. It is a quiet island that is known more for its natural attractions.

One major road along the coast circles the island and the volcano, which allows visitors to reach various attractions quickly and easily. Because of the volcano, a large part of the island is not easy to visit except for the most fit and adventurous cruise visitors.

The Brimstone Hill Fortress National Park, a well-preserved fort dating back to 1690, is a UNESCO World Heritage Site. Brimstone is one of the best preserved forts in the Caribbean. It is 30 minutes northwest of the cruise docks and available as a shore excursion.

Nearby Beaches

St. Kitts is not known for its beaches, but it has several within driving distance of Basseterre. If taking a taxi to the beach, be sure to ask for rates before getting into a cab.

Some cruise lines offer Frigate Bay as a shore excursion. It has a one-mile stretch of white sand and many activities including windsurfing and waterskiing. It also has nearby bars and restaurants.

South Friars Bay on the Caribbean side of the island is a popular choice with local amenities. More active visitors might prefer North Friars Bay on the Atlantic side. It has a much stronger surf.

Anyone thinking about seeing Brimstone Hill Fortress can combine that trip with a visit to the black sands of Pump Bay beach.

Shopping / Restaurants

The port has two docks, but the newer and more popular dock is Port Zande.

Visitors will immediately see exhibits, displays and cruise operators as they walk off the ship.

Right past this point is the Zande duty-free shopping area, which offers fine jewelry, liquor and souvenirs and restaurants.

Next is Pelican Mall, the ground floor of which houses the headquarters of the St. Kitts Tourism Authority. Stop there for any questions about things to see and do on the island.

Also nearby are the National Museum and the Circus, an octagonal plaza that is similar to a miniature version of London's famous Piccadilly Circus.

In the center of the Circus is the Berkeley Memorial Drinking Fountain and Clock, erected in 1891. Around the edge is more duty-free shops, banks and restaurants.

Getting Around / Transportation

The St. Kitts cruise port is a walking destination. The mall area is massive, and it's right next to Basseterre. So a few hours of walking to shop, dine and view local attractions is a given.
Taxi rates are posted rather than metered. Each location on the island has a specific fare.

A car rental is a good idea for any cruise visitors with enough time to spare because St. Kitts has a number of decent attractions around the island.

Like other destinations, most of the car rental agencies cluster around Basseterre and next to the nearby airport.

Most of the agencies are locally owned. At least two international companies have a presence -- Avis and Thrifty.

However, drivers need a permit that costs $24. Cruise visitors who plan to visit more than one attractions around the county may find that renting a car is less expensive than taking two separate tour buses.

Weather / Best Times to Go

St. Kitts lies close to Antigua and St. Maarten and shares common weather patterns.

Average monthly high temperatures range between the low 80s Fahrenheit in the winter to the upper 80s in the summer. They make the island a warm destination year round.

Rain is moderate except for a brief rainy season in May and a spike in rainfall in September through November during the annual Caribbean hurricane season.

As such, eastern Caribbean cruises that include St. Kitts hit a high point from December through March during the dry season. They reach a low point in the fall during the a time of heavier rains.

St. Lucia: Castries

Eastern and Southern Caribbean

The St. Lucia cruise port of Castries is one of the prettiest in the Caribbean. If the flowers are in bloom, all the better.

The Castries Harbor is really a snug inlet surrounded by hills like a deep comfortable blanket.

Wait until the ship arrives and then walk out onto the deck for the best and most fulfilling view of the trees, water and docks. The main sea port is Castries and many cruise ships anchor at Pointe Seraphine and La Place Carenage.

Mist hangs over the greens hills in the interior of St. Lucia.

Quick Tips

- St. Lucia is known for beaches, scenery and outdoor attractions.
- Outside of Castries, check out Reduit Beach and the Pitons.
- Taxis closest to the docks tend to charge the most. Negotiate price.

Attractions and Shore Excursions

St. Lucia is a fairly large island at 238 square miles. It offers plenty of space to explore.

The first attraction for any cruise visitor is the Pointe Seraphine Duty Free Shopping Complex right by the cruise docks. Like most popular Caribbean destinations, it is an open-air mall with several dozen shops selling jewelry, perfume, car rentals, excursions, clothing, liquor and food.

The city itself has a few other attractions worth noting. Derek Walcott Square, named after the Nobel winner from St. Lucia, is another gathering place for shoppers. It is one mile southeast of the cruise docks.

Cathedral Basilica of the Immaculate Conception, Micoud Street and Laborie Street at Walcott Square, is a picturesque photo opportunity of one of the largest churches in the West Indies.

Fort Charlotte, which is now a college, was the site of some of extensive fighting between the French and the British. The Choiseul Heritage site is a village with history, crafts and island views.

Otherwise, the rest of St. Lucia outside of Castries emphasizes nature.

Soufrière is both a village and home of St. Lucia's most famous landmark, the Pitons, a pair of dormant volcanoes more than 2,000 feet high. It is a common cruise excursion.

Visitors hike up the mountains and take volcanic mud baths for their reputed restorative powers.

Anyone who wants a gentler nature excursion can take a rain forest tram, another cruise line excursion. The open-air gondolas hold eight passengers and a nature guide. It is a three-hour excursion for less than $100 per person.

Pigeon Island, a destination for some cruise line excursions, has been the home of the Amerindians, a pirate hideout and a military base. It also has a beach. It is about 25 minutes north of Castries and is actually accessible by car.

Fond Doux Estate is a Caribbean-style working plantation has a variety of tropical fruits and plants.

Families or people with less time or energy can take advantage of St. Lucia's beauty on the Tet Paul Nature Trail, a 45-minute hike near Soufrière.

The hike has views of Jalousie Bay and Gros Piton as well as the islands of Martinique and St. Vincent. It also has an organic farm, traditional house and exotic horticulture.

Anyone renting a car might explore the fishing villages of Anse-La-Raye and Canaries.

Nearby Beaches

Reduit Beach at Rodney Bay, about 10 miles north of Castries, is the longest and one of the most popular beaches on the island.

Next to Reduit is Pigeon Island National Park, a popular spot for snorkeling and scuba diving.

Grande Anse lies on the east coast of the island and is a few miles farther from Castries as Reduit. It is a popular beach for turtle watching.

Eight miles south of Castries is Anse Chastanet, another popular beach known for long stretches of white sand and some areas of black volcanic sand. It also has good snorkeling and scuba diving. Smaller nearby beaches for anyone with limited time include Vigie, La Toc and Malabar.

Shopping / Restaurants

Duty-free shopping is located at La Place Carenage and the Spanish-style complex of Pointe Seraphine. Goods include fine china, crystal, perfume and leather products.

Designer jewelry and watch brands include Caribbean Hook, Honora, John Atencio, John Hardy, Kabana, Roberto Coin, Starnight, Alfex, Cartier, Concord, Gucci, Maurice LaCroix, Michèle, Movado and Wenger.

An outdoor market on Jeremie Street has a wide array of straw goods. The best known products are the hand-silk-screened and hand-printed fabrics and fashions created by local craftsmen.

A variety of shopping malls with extended opening hours offer a wide selection of boutiques and restaurants. Most hotels have boutiques and vendors' markets.

Local shops are generally open weekdays from 8.30 a.m. to 4 p.m. and on Saturday 8 a.m. to noon.

Higher-end restaurants in Castries or nearby include Tao, Foggie Jacks, Coal Pot at Vigie Marina and Rainforest Hideaway. Fast food restaurants include Domino's Pizza, Burger King and Burger Plus.

Getting Around / Transportation

Roads outside of Castries are limited, so plan on taking extra time to get to the most popular beaches and attractions.

Taxis have standard fares for common destinations rather than metered fares. Always ask for the fare before getting into the taxi.

Minibuses serve as the main public ground transportation for the island. Buses run at varied times depending on the route.

There is no scheduled bus timetable. Bus fares from Castries to the north end of the island is EC $2.50. From Castries to the south end of the island (Vieux Fort) is EC $8.

Car travel via the new West Coast Road from Castries to Soufriere takes about an hour.

Major car rental agencies include Avis, Budget, Hertz and National.

Weather / Best Times to Go

Anyone planning to go to St. Lucia on a cruise or thinking about going should know what to expect with the weather.

The island's average high temperature ranges from the low 80s Fahrenheit in January and February to the mid to high 80s for the rest of the year.
Rainfall varies greatly month to month. The island receives about three to four inches of rain from December through June.

It starts to climb in July during the Caribbean hurricane season and reaches a high point of eight inches in September and October.

St. Maarten: Philipsburg

Eastern and Southern Caribbean

A St. Maarten cruise has great appeal simply because the island has one of the best cruise ports in the entire Caribbean.

What makes a good cruise port arguably is a combination of:

- Shopping
- Beaches
- Excursions
- Local people
- Atmosphere

St. Maarten visitors walk off the ships and into the cruise mall.

The St. Maarten cruise port of Philipsburg has all of the above in a pleasant mix. It is a must-see stop for any southern or eastern Caribbean cruise and why 2 million cruise visitors tour the port every year.

Quick Tips

- The main St. Maarten cruise port is Dr. A.C. Wathey Cruise & Cargo Facilities at Philipsburg.
- Walk a half mile, drive or take a water taxi to the city.
- Great Bay Beach and shopping on Front Street run side by side.
- Orient Beach and Marigot are two popular attractions on the French side of the island.

Attractions and Shore Excursions

Philipsburg itself is one of the best attractions on the island because of its appealing and well-developed tourism district.

It is rare among Caribbean ports to have a decent beach right by the city. Great Bay Beach has a long boardwalk with bars and restaurants. Running parallel to the boardwalk is Front Street, which has most of the shops.

Orient Beach, which lies north of Philipsburg in the French district, is the most popular and well-known beach on the island. Note that it is clothing optional. Don't be surprised to see a beach goer who wears nothing at all.

One of the more famous and controversial attractions is the Maho Bay beach next to Princess Juliana International Airport. The short runway forces planes to fly low over the beach. Some beach visitors get so close that the blast from the jet engines knock them over.

A nice day trip is a jaunt from the Philipsburg cruise port over to Marigot, capital of the French side, or Grand Case. Other St. Maarten attractions include the Mont Vernon Plantation and the Butterfly Farm.

Nearby Beaches

Philipsburg has that convenient beach right there by the cruise docks on Great Bay. Cruise visitors who arrive from the docks by foot, taxi or water taxi will get dropped off right by the Great Bay Beach.

They can rent umbrellas and chairs for a reasonable price and a lovely view of bay.

Orient Bay, a well-known clothing-optional beach on the French side, is easy to reach via tour bus or other means. That makes this destination appealing for cruise visitors, but otherwise most of the beaches are small and scattered.

Anyone with an interest in good beaches might try an excursion to one of the neighboring islands, such as Anguilla, St. Barts or Saba.

Anguilla is the most popular of the three. It has beautiful white sand beaches and is reachable by ferry from Simpson Bay and Marigot. St. Barts is frequented by the rich and famous. Saba is known for hiking and other ecotourism activities.

Adding to the experience of a St. Maarten cruise visit is the friendliness of the local people, whether while shopping, touring or taking a bus. It is one reason why the St. Maarten tourism slogan is "The Friendly Island."

The combination of the above experiences creates an atmosphere that will be memorable for cruise visitors.

Shopping / Restaurants

Anyone wanting a break from Great Bay Beach can walk a few more feet to reach the Boardwalk, which is lined with restaurants and shops.

They can walk a hundred more feet to reach many more restaurants and the port's extensive shopping district, most of which falls along the lengthy Front Street.

Front Street ranks among one of the best shopping experiences in the Caribbean -- along with Playa Del Carmen, St. Thomas and Old San Juan. It is a festive pedestrian beach.

The street is a long walk but not too challenging for anyone who is somewhat fit. If walking isn't appealing, there are quite a few transportation options.

Restaurants are mainly concentrated in two areas -- Philipsburg on the southern coast and Simpson Bay on the southwest coast because they have the cruise port and the airport.

More restaurants sit in the packed resort areas. A smaller number of restaurants are on the French side in Marigot and Grand Case.

The Philipsburg and Simpson Bay restaurants cater to all tastes, but they mainly represent low-end casual in one group and high-end seafood and steak in the other.

There are few chain restaurants. The St. Martin French restaurants tend to be smaller and casual in Marigot.

Getting Around / Transportation

On foot. Philipsburg is big enough and developed enough to spend most of the day on foot.

But traffic outside of the Boardwalk and Front Street is often heavy. So get a taxi or car rental if you plan to see more than just the tourism district.

Taxis. Taxi rates are set according to more than 20 zones around the island.

Expect to pay anywhere between $7 and $35 to get to a zone. At the time of this writing, getting to Marigot is $18 and Orient Beach is $20.

Car rentals. The island has a small number of narrow winding roads, so car rentals even for a day are quite common -- so common that traffic jams are frequent.

A cruise visitor who is thinking about a car rental might do so for visits to the less-populated French side of the island, especially the quaint city of Marigot.

Driving around parts of the Dutch side, especially around Simpson Bay, adds some risk of traffic jams and late returns to the ship.

Public bus. Taking a bus is a less expensive option. A St. Maarten bus is often an SUV. It has BUS at the beginning of the license plate and the destination sign in the window.

Taxis, which also are usually SUVs, have a T at the beginning of the license plate. A 10-15 percent tip for bus and taxi drivers is common.

Bicycles / scooters. While it is useful to consider a rental car, bus or taxi, it is wise to avoid renting a bicycle or scooter.

The island has few stop signs or stop lights. The roads are narrow and winding. Drivers are sometimes aggressive when fighting through traffic.

St. Maarten's average weather consists of warm temperatures year round that average in the mid 80s Fahrenheit.

Sea water averages about three degrees cooler, which makes swimming good at any time.
Rainfall is a different matter. It is often moderate from January through July. Then it climbs to a high point for the rest of the year.

September and November historically have the highest rainfall and are the riskiest months to go there.

St. Thomas: U.S. Virgin Islands

Eastern Caribbean

The St. Thomas cruise port at Charlotte Amalie is one of the most popular duty-free shopping destinations in the Caribbean. It's also a common stop for any eastern Caribbean cruise.

More than 2 million people visit the U.S. Virgin Islands by cruise ship every year, according to the Caribbean Tourism Organization. The vast majority go to St. Thomas. The fact that St. Thomas is so popular with cruises makes it a very commercialized experience.

Ships usually disembark passengers at the Havensight cruise dock. Visitors can walk off the ship and right into Havensight Mall, which has more than 100 shops and the same duty-free prices as Charlotte Amalie.

The mall area has grown to the point where fewer visitors are going into Charlotte Amalie to shop. It's possible to limit shopping to the dock area, forget about Charlotte Amalie and take off for attractions and excursions.

Quick Tips

- Charlotte Amalie is a long walk or short taxi ride from the docks.
- Duty-free shopping limit is double most other Caribbean islands.
- Attractions are OK, beaches are good, snorkeling is great.

Sailboats fill the harbor at Charlotte Amalie.

Attractions and Shore Excursions

St. Thomas cruise visitors can take advantage of other things to do besides shopping and dining at the many outdoor restaurants.

The island does not have famous natural attractions like other islands, such as Stingray City at Grand Cayman. But it does have well-known commercial attractions.

One of them is right by the cruise docks. The St. Thomas Skyride near Havensight Mall goes 700 feet up to the top of Flag Hill for a grander view of Charlotte Amalie and St. Thomas Harbor. Photographers have plenty of views to shoot. Tickets at the time of this writing were $21 for teens and adults and $10.50 for children 12 and under.

The Coral World Marine Park and Observatory at Coki Point has a tropical nature trail, marine gardens aquarium, coral reef tank and an underwater observatory. It's a 25 minute drive on the opposite side of the island from the cruise docks. General admission tickets are $10 for adults and $6 for children. Animal encounters cost more; prices vary.

Historical attractions include Fort Christian, the oldest structure in the Virgin Islands and dating from the early 1670s. It is one and a half miles from the docks and within Charlotte Amalie. Passengers can combine a visit to the fort along with some shopping.

Blackbeard's Castle, a watch tower built in 1679, is the focal point for a tourist attraction that includes a garden, rum factory, hotel and other facilities. The site at Lille Taarne Gade is just a five minute walk north of Fort Christian.

Nearby Beaches

Some cruise visitors just like to hit a good beach.

Visitors can jump into a taxi and spend the afternoon at the nearest beaches, which are Limestone and Morningstar.

Limestone is small and quiet, while Morningstar is larger and more active. Two resorts overlook Morningstar, which makes it easier to get a taxi back to the cruise ship.

Magens Bay is St. Thomas's most popular beach. The one-mile-long beach is a public park with calm waters protected by a heart-shaped bay. It is only four miles north of the docks and a quick ride by taxi, rental car or excursion bus.

Beach chairs and floats are available for rent. Burgers, pizzas and other snacks are available for sale at the snack bar. Lifeguards are on duty every day.

Coki Beach, located at Coki Point next to Coral World Ocean Park, is popular for snorkeling and diving. Services include food vendors, dive shop, jet ski rental, beach chairs and floats.

Shopping / Restaurants

Shopping

Anyone with a big interest in shopping can start at Havensight Mall first and then move on to the town.

Otherwise, the mall is a quick and easy shopping option for visitors planning other activities during their cruise visit.

Walking to Charlotte Amalie from the ship and the mall is an option for very fit people with extra time; a taxi is a more likely option. Taxi rates are based on the destination, per person, and are not metered.

Expect to pay about $8-10 to go from the dock to the town. As always, check the rate with the driver before entering the vehicle.

Charlotte Amalie shops have many of the same goods as the mall -- jewelry, gemstones, watches, designer clothing and spirits -- but there are many more shops and chance for more bargains.

Most of the stores are on Main Street. The duty-free allowance is $1,600.

Restaurants

Both Havensight Mall and Charlotte Amalie town have a wide assortment of casual restaurants. U.S. dollars, credit cards and traveler's checks are widely accepted.

Havensight Mall restaurants include Beni Iguana's Sushi Bar and Restaurant, Barefoot Buddha (sandwiches), Havensight Café, Hooters, Paradise Gate, Paradise Point Bar and Café, Senor Frogs, The Delly Deck and The Great Wall Chinese Restaurant.

Charlotte Amalie restaurants include Big Kahuna Rum Shack, Coconuts Bar and Grill, Cuzzin's Caribbean Restaurant, Gladys Café, Golden Dragon Chinese, Hervé Restaurant and Wine Bar Restaurant, Jen's Gourmet Café and Deli, The Greenhouse Restaurant and Virgilio's Restaurant.

Getting Around / Transportation

Taxis on St. Thomas are not metered. The Virgin Islands Taxicab Division sets rates, which are per person and per destination.

Expect to pay about $8-10 per person for two people to take a taxi from the cruise docks to Charlotte Amalie. Always check the rate with the driver before getting into the cab.

Many car rental agencies are on the island, mainly concentrated at the airport. But they usually provide free pickup and dropoff.

Limited bus routes also are available but not recommended.

Weather / Best Times to Go

Warm weather isn't a problem for the U.S. Virgin Islands.

The average high temperature ranges from 85 degrees Fahrenheit from December through March to about 90 degrees from July through September.

Rainfall determines the best time to go. The islands average two to three inches of rain per month from December through July.

Heavier rains begin in August and reach a high point of more than five inches in September, October and November during the peak of the Caribbean hurricane season.

Turks and Caicos: Cockburn Town

Eastern Caribbean

The Grand Turk cruise port on the southern tip of the island is not a city like most cruise ports. It is a separate cruise center built by Carnival.

It seems a logical thing to do on a small island of only 4,500 people. The island lies midway between the Bahamas and better known locations to the south.

As a result of its location, Grand Turk has become a common stop among eastern Caribbean cruise ports for Carnival and other cruise ships.

Turks and Caicos Islands are a British Overseas Territory. The islands are 30 miles south of the Bahamas and just to the north of Dominican Republic. Grand Turk is one of 40 islands that form the Turks and Caicos archipelago. The island is about seven miles long and one and a half miles wide, which makes it easy to tour by bus, taxi or even bicycle.

Quick Tips

- The Grand Turk Cruise Center is a 18-acre welcome facility.
- The center has a pool and beaches within walking distance.
- Nearby Cockburn Town is the island's capital and historic district.

Attractions and Shore Excursions

Visitors will walk off the dock and onto the 18-acre cruise center complex. It has not only a beach and pool but also dining, shopping excursions, car rentals, taxis and buses. Shopping of course is duty free.

A FlowRider is one of the newer attractions. The complex also has a 45,000 square foot shopping center with 10,000 square feet of duty free shopping. So cruise passengers can spend the entire day there or spend a little time and take off for other things to do.

Once cruise visitors pass through the cruise center at the southern tip of the island -- if they ever do because of the variety of available activities -- they have to take a taxi or excursion bus to reach Cockburn Town.

The town with a population of 3,700 people has more shopping and dining plus a national museum.

It is known for its 18th and 19th architecture along Duke and Front streets along with winding roads and old street lamps.

Otherwise, Grand Turk is not known for the kind of popular and unique attractions that inhabit some other Caribbean islands.

Cruise line excursions make up the most common things to do outside of the cruise center, beaches and Cockburn Town.

Whale watching. Whale watching trips are available from late January through early April to see North Atlantic Humpback Whales take part in their annual migration and mating habits.

The Grand Turk Lighthouse at the northern tip of the island is a working lighthouse. Visitors can picnic in the shade and watch whales during the migration season.

Land Excursions. Provo Golf Club is an 18-hole residential and community golf course that hosted the 2009 Caribbean Amateur Golf Championship.

Excursion operators have 4x4 safaris, helicopter rides, horseback rides with swim and dune buggy rides.

Water excursions. Snorkeling and diving are popular thanks to a reef that is 200 miles long and 65 miles wide. It has an 8,000 foot drop off. It is close enough to the shore for beach dives.

Excursion operators at the cruise center offer snorkeling with the stingrays, catamaran sailing, parasailing, deep sea fishing tours and bottom fishing tours.

Passengers can interact with stingrays at Gibbs Cay island. The attraction is a common cruise line excursion.

Nearby Beaches

The cruise center has 1,000 feet of beachfront. South Beach also is available for anyone who wants a quieter experience.

Two more beaches lie within walking distance -- Governor's Beach to the north and White Sands Beach to the south.

Anyone planning to see Cockburn Town, the Grand Turk Lighthouse (three miles north of town) or other attractions will find more beaches near both the cruise center and the town.

They include Cedar Grove Beach and Town Beach. Beaches north of the town include West Road, Pillory and Cocktree.

Shopping / Restaurants

Visitors disembarking at the Grand Turk Cruise Center will find restaurants available in the center.

They include a Jimmy Buffett's "Margaritaville" restaurant. Other restaurants outside the cruise center include:

Guanahani Restaurant & Bar in Bohio Resort, open for breakfast lunch and dinner with a menu that is both local and international.
Osprey Beach Hotel, 1 Duke Street, with fresh fish, the catch of the day, lobster in season, as well as steaks, lamb and chicken.

Manta House on Duke Street is a beach bar open for lunch and dinner.

The U.S. dollar is the official currency. Most shops and restaurants will accept traveler's checks. All of the cruise center stores accept credit cards.

Getting Around / Transportation

Tony's Car Rental in the cruise center offers car, scooter and bicycle rentals. Grand Turk is small enough that bike riders can reach Cockburn Town and other locations. The town is three miles from the cruise center; there are no sidewalks.

Taxi fares are not metered. They are set in advance with fares listed on posted signs. The taxi stand is in the cruise center behind the shops.

Grand Turk Taxi Association has tariffs based on four island zones named A. B, C and D. One-way rates from the cruise center range from $4 to $9 per person depending on the destination. The cruise center is in zone A while Cockburn Town is in Zone B.

Weather

Turks and Caicos has some of the most sunshine and least amount of rain in the Caribbean. Government officials say it has 350 days of sunshine every year. (But "sunshine" also includes some clouds.)

The average temperature ranges between 80 and 90 degrees from June to October, according to Turks and Caicos Tourism. On some days, temperatures reach into the mid 90s.

Average temperatures hover in the low 80s Fahrenheit from November to May. Water temperatures will often dip into the low 70s. They may feel chilly for swimming if trade winds are strong.

Total rainfall is similar to Aruba, Bonaire and Curacao farther south. Rainfall for Grand Turk averages less than two inches a month. It climbs higher during the Caribbean hurricane season in September and October.

Embarkation Ports

About U.S. Ports to the Caribbean

Choosing a U.S. cruise port as the starting point of a cruise vacation is an important decision that can save time and money.

Anyone who lives within a reasonable distance of a cruise port will find that driving there often is less expensive than flying there.

The price of airline tickets depends heavily on the distance between the starting point and the embarkation port. The closer the port, the cheaper the price.

The Caribbean is the most active cruise region in the world, and the Florida cruise ports are the most active embarkation ports in the world. They also have benefits before and after a cruise such as more beaches, more warm weather and plenty of their own attractions for travelers who have extra time available.

The best time to visit Florida for good weather is in the spring because rainfall increases quite a bit in the summer. But the cruise ports are busy most of the year.

Many newcomers to cruises don't often know that major cruise lines also embark from many cities along the Gulf Coast and East Coast in addition to Florida.

Florida Cruise Ports

Florida has three major cruise ports at Miami, Fort Lauderdale and Port Canaveral near Orlando. It also has two smaller ports at Tampa and

Jacksonville. Ships embarking from Florida often go to all three major regions in the Caribbean -- eastern, western and southern.

Miami is the busiest cruise port in the world and home to ships of the largest cruise lines including Carnival, Norwegian and Royal Caribbean. The city also has the widest range of cultural activities and offers plenty of beachfront as well.

Fort Lauderdale is the next busiest and has many departing ships from the Princess and Holland America cruise lines. Like Miami, Fort Lauderdale is known for its beaches and also has many cultural attractions.

The Florida port with the most famous and popular nearby attractions is Port Canaveral on the east coast. It lies close to the Kennedy Space Center at Cape Canaveral and is about a one-hour drive from Orlando, home of Disneyworld and Universal Studios. Carnival, Disney and Royal Caribbean have ships that embark from there.

Tampa is the only cruise port on the western coast of Florida and is becoming more active as a starting destination. Cruise lines operating from there include Carnival, Norwegian, Holland America and Royal Caribbean.

Jacksonville is the most northern port in Florida -- located near the border with Georgia -- and has a limited number of Carnival cruises that embark from there. Most of the cruises are short-term visits to the Bahamas.

Gulf Coast Cruise Ports

Tampa is both a Florida and Gulf Coast cruise port. Besides Tampa, New Orleans and especially Galveston Texas are active embarkation ports for

Caribbean cruises.

Their location makes them more appealing to anyone living in western Canada and the United States who will find that driving or flying there takes less time (and is cheaper) than going to Florida.

Galveston is home to ships from Carnival and Royal Caribbean. A large number of cruises go to western Caribbean ports such as Cozumel, Costa Maya, Jamaica, Roatan, Belize and Grand Cayman.

New Orleans is active mostly with Carnival Cruise Lines and offers quite a few shorter cruises to the western Caribbean.

Houston Texas also has a cruise port located near Galveston. It is home to ships from the Prince and Norwegian cruise lines.

East Coast Cruise Ports

Some of the largest cities on the eastern coast of the United States are active cruise embarkation ports for Bermuda, the Bahamas, the Caribbean, New England and Canada.

Caribbean cruises from those destinations usually go to the Bahamas and the northernmost islands in the eastern Caribbean.

Those ports include Baltimore, Cape Liberty New Jersey, New York City, Norfolk Virginia and Savannah Georgia.

Baltimore has ships from Carnival and Royal Caribbean. New York City has cruise ships from Carnival and Norwegian. Cape Liberty has a limited number of cruises by Royal Caribbean. Norfolk and Savannah also have a limited number of cruises.

Baltimore, New York City and Cape Liberty, which is right by New York

City, all have easy access to major cultural attractions. Norfolk is known for its nearby Virginia Beach and closeness to Washington D.C. and major historical attractions in Virginia.

Baltimore, Maryland

Baltimore may not sound like a starting point for a Caribbean cruise to anyone who is new to cruises.

But the capital of Maryland does act as a port of embarkation for cruises to Bermuda, the Bahamas, the Bahamas, Canada and New England. Because it is far north on the East Coast, it mostly sends ships to Bermuda, fewer to the Bahamas and even fewer to the Caribbean.

The port is home to ships from American, Carnival, Crystal and Royal Caribbean cruise lines. More than a quarter of a million cruise travelers start their trip from it each year, according to the Maryland Port Administration.

The city is growing as an embarkation point because it is located within a six-hour drive of 40 million people, the Administration says. It is the closest East Coast port for drivers from Pittsburgh, Cleveland, Indianapolis and Chicago and is a three-hour drive from the New York City metro area.

The terminal opens at 8 a.m. or two hours after the ship arrives. Passengers need a cruise ticket and a valid passport to enter the terminal building.

Passengers must arrive for check-in at least 90 minutes to two hours before the ship is scheduled to depart. This arrival time will allow the cruise line to process them and have them on board at least 60 minutes before departure. Late passengers may be denied boarding.

Nearby Attractions

The Cruise Maryland terminal is 2.5 miles from Inner Harbor, the Baltimore development with restaurants, shopping and entertainment.

Attractions include the National Aquarium, 501 Pratt Street; USS Constellation, 301 E. Pratt Street; and Pratt Street Power Plant, an historic dining and entertainment venue at 601 E. Pratt Street. The B&O Railroad Museum is located at 901 W. Pratt Street.

Inner Harbor is a pleasant and pretty experience especially during good weather.

For anyone with less time, Fort McHenry, 2400 East Fort Avenue, is 1.6 miles from the terminal. The fort is famous for the 1814 attack by the British while Francis Scott Key wrote "The Star-Spangled Banner".

Location and Directions

The Cruise Maryland terminal is 10 miles from BWI Thurgood Marshall Airport on the Patapsco River near Inner Harbor and Fort McHenry. The terminal is easily accessible from I-95.

Anyone taking I-95 North should get off the highway at exit 55, also known as Key Highway. Continue straight for less than one mile on East McComas Street. The terminal entrance is on the right.

Anyone taking I-95 South should stay in the far right lane (bore #1) when going through the Fort McHenry tunnel. Take Exit 55 at Key Highway. Turn left at the traffic light onto East McComas Street. The terminal will be about 350 feet on the right.

Visitors driving toward the port from the west on I-70 East should merge onto I-695 South at Exit 91A. Go 5.2 miles and merge onto I-95 North via Exit 11A. Continue on I-95 North for about 4.9 miles to Exit 55, Key Highway. Keep driving straight for less than one mile on East McComas Street. The terminal entrance is on the right.

Parking

Parking is $15 per night for passenger cars, $30 for recreational vehicles under 30 feet and $40 for recreational vehicles over 30 feet. Prices are subject to change.

Parking rates are payable after arrival with cash, credit cards, or traveler's checks. The terminal accepts VISA, MasterCard, and American Express.

Weather

Baltimore is one of the northernmost ports that send ships to Bermuda, the Bahamas and the Caribbean.

So it's no surprise that it's one of the coldest during the winter. As a result, it usually has cruises mostly during the summer.

The average high temperatures in the summer reach 90 degrees Fahrenheit. Rainfall is modest at three to four inches a month from June through August.

Cape Liberty, New Jersey

The Cape Liberty cruise port doesn't hold the same status as Miami, but it has been the starting point for more than 300,000 people going on cruises.

The port opened in 2004 on The Peninsula at Bayonne Harbor in Bayonne, New Jersey. It is a former naval base located 15 minutes from the Newark Liberty International Airport and seven miles south of Manhattan.

Because of its location, it has views and easy access to the Statue of Liberty and New York Harbor in addition to Manhattan.

It is the home port of ships from Royal Caribbean and Celebrity Cruises that sail to Bermuda, the Bahamas, Canada, New England, eastern Caribbean and southern Caribbean.

The Peninsula At Bayonne Harbor is in the middle of a transformation from an abandoned military base into a 430-acre, mixed-use development including retail, dining, entertainment and the cruise facility.

The facility opens at 10:30 a.m. on the day of the cruise. All passengers must arrive at least 90 minutes before boarding time. Terminal doors will close 90 minutes before departure. Anyone arriving later will not be able to board the ship.

Passengers should complete their online pre-registrations at least six days before departure. Anyone who does not complete pre-registration must arrive at least two hours before departing or else will not be allowed to board. On arrival, passengers must have passports or government IDs ready for security clearance.

More information about the port is available at its Web site. The address is cruiseliberty.com.

Nearby Attractions

The fact that the Statue of Liberty is viewable from the cruise port makes it an obvious attraction for anyone with a car and some extra time on their hands. The statue is about seven miles northeast of the port via I-78 or major urban roads depending on traffic.

Lower Manhattan is about 10 miles away and may take about 30 minutes to reach. It has the Soho District, Battery Park, the September 11 Memorial, World Trade Center site and Castle Clinton National Monument.

Midtown Manhattan requires a longer drive, but it offers several of the most famous attractions in New York including the Empire State Building, Central Park and Times Square.

Visitors can take one of three highway options: I-78 east from Newark Liberty International Airport, I-95 south to I-78 or I-95 north to I-78. Anyone taking I-95 to I-78 will go then go east to the New Jersey Turnpike.

Once on the turnpike, take exit 14-A off the turnpike and follow the signs for Route 440 South. Drive 1.5 miles and turn left into the Bayonne Ocean Terminal. The cruise terminal is two miles ahead.

The address is 14 Port Terminal Boulevard, Bayonne, NJ 07002.

Parking

The parking facility is located adjacent to the cruise terminal. Parking fees are $20 per day including state and local sales tax. Prices are subject to change.

Travelers do not need to make reservations. The facility accepts cash, travelers cheques and major credit cards.

Weather

Cape Liberty has the kind of weather most people will expect for a location in New Jersey. It's cold and snowy during the winter and warm during the summer. This is definitely a summertime cruise port unless a ship is going very south.

The average high temperature during the summer reaches into the mid 80s Fahrenheit or nearly 30 Celsius. Average highs in the winter drop into the low 40s Fahrenheit or single digits Celsius.

Precipitation -- both rain and snow -- stays within a tight range throughout the year. The total is about three to four inches a month.

Charleston, South Carolina

Charleston South Carolina is both a popular place to visit on its own and an active starting point for Caribbean cruises.

The city is known for dining, history and architecture. Port of Charleston is in the historic district, which makes it easy for passengers to see the best city sights before or after their cruise.

Ships embarking from Charleston include Carnival Fantasy, Carnival Ecstasy and Seven Seas Mariner. Common cruise destinations include Nassau Bahamas, Turks and Caicos, and Amber Cove Dominican Republic.

Nearby Attractions

The historic district is a great place for simply walking around to view the mansions and historic buildings. Other nearby attractions include the South Carolina Aquarium and The Citadel military college.

Fort Sumter is the most famous Charleston attraction. It is about 11 miles from the cruise terminal, so visitors will need a taxi, rental car or tour bus to get there.

Other attractions include City Market, Middleton Place, Magnolia Place and Gardens, Waterfront Park, Drayton Hall, Boone Hall and Charles Towne Landing.

Location and Directions

The port is easily accessible from I-26, Highway 17 North and Highway 17 South. Be aware of highway signs providing directions to the cruise terminal.

From I-26 west, take exit 219 B and go left on Mount Pleasant Street. Continue through two intersections and onto Morrison Drive / Route 52. Continue south under the bridge until Morrison becomes East Bay Street. Go left on Chapel Street, left on Charlotte Street, right on Concord Street to Union Pier Terminal Gate 2.

From I-26 east, take the same exit 219 B and turn left at the foot of the exit ramp. Cross King and Meeting streets to Morrison Drive and follow the same directions above.

Gate 2 at the intersection of Concord and Laurens streets is the entrance for passengers in personal vehicles. It is the gate for anyone planning to park at the terminal or being dropped off there.

Cruise travelers can park their vehicles and process luggage starting at noon and continuing until 3 p.m. Passengers should go to the luggage collection site before checking in to the cruise.

Parking

Parking costs $20 a day for standard-sized vehicles and $50 per day for oversized vehicles such as campers and buses. Prices are subject to change. Vehicles displaying a valid handicap permit, handicap license plate and valid ID receive free parking for their cruise. The person with the handicap permit must be traveling in the vehicle.

Assistance is also available at the Port drop off areas for guests not storing vehicles. Complimentary shuttle service is provided for all passengers between the Port parking areas and the Passenger Terminal.

Passengers must show cruise line documents and photo ID to board the shuttle buses. Credit cards, cash, traveler's check, or personal check (payable to SCSPA) will be accepted as payment. Checks written on non-U.S. banks and financial institutions are not accepted.

Payment is due when vehicle is left in storage on departure day of the cruise.

Weather

Charleston is farther south than Baltimore or New York, but it has similar temperatures during the summer. The average highs get into the upper 80s Fahrenheit, according to the U.S. National Weather Service.

But the city gets more rain than Baltimore or New York. Rain is especially heavy from July through September when it averages six to seven inches a month. That makes Charleston a better embarkation port in late spring to early summer.

Fort Lauderdale, Florida

The Port Everglades cruise terminal is not located in the Florida Everglades, but rather in nearby Fort Lauderdale. The alligators are relieved.

The port is one of the top three cruise ports in the world, according to the Broward County Port Everglades Department. It supports 10 cruise lines, 44 ships, nine terminals and more than 4 million cruise passengers a year.

Caribbean cruise visitors will find that reaching the port and starting their vacation is fairly simple because the port, airport and major highways are all close together.

Nearby Attractions

Families with time on their hands may want to visit the Museum of Discovery and Science at 401 SW Second Street in Fort Lauderdale. The museum has a variety of special and permanent exhibits as well as an Imax movie theater.

Beach lovers should consider John U. Lloyd Beach State Park at 6503 N Ocean Dr, Dania Beach, about eight miles south of the port. (Be sure not to go during rush hour traffic.) The park offers swimming, surf fishing, canoeing, nature study, boating and picnicking.

The 35-acre Bonnet House, 900 Birch Road, is a museum and garden on the U.S. National Register of Historic Places. It is six miles from the port.

Location and Directions

Fort Lauderdale-Hollywood International Airport is the main airport serving the cruise port. It is located less than two miles away.

Many car rental agencies are available at the airport in its Rental Car Center. It takes about 45 minutes to transfer from the airport to the cruise port.

Other airports serving the Port Everglades include Miami International Airport (27 miles south) and Palm Beach International Airport (50 miles north).

For taxis, expect to pay between $10 and $15 for transportation between Fort Lauderdale-Hollywood International Airport and Port Everglades. Expect to pay about $18 to $20 for a taxi ride between the port and downtown Fort Lauderdale.

Transfers are usually included for anyone who has bought an air and sea travel package.

Broward County Transit offers local bus service. The Tri-Rail commuter train is available in Broward, Miami-Dade and Palm Beach counties.

Parking

Parking is available for cruise passengers in the Northport and Midport Parking Garages and the Northport and Midport Surface Lots, according to the Broward County Port Everglades Department.

Garage and surface parking rates are the same. Car fees have a daily maximum of $15. Prices are subject to change. Pay with cash or major credit card.

The Northport Parking Garage services Cruise Terminals 1, 2 and 4. The Northpoint Surface Lot is dedicated to terminal 4.

To reach them, turn south on Eisenhower Boulevard from 17th Street Causeway or travel east on State Road 84, enter the Port and turn left at Eisenhower.

From I-595, go east all the way into the Port. Follow the signs for Terminals #1, 2 & 4 and/or the Convention Center.

The Midport garage services cruise terminals 19, 21, 22/24, 25, 26, 27 and 29. To reach it, take I-595 east into the Port. Continue east to the garage on the left side of the street.

The Midport Surface Lots service Cruise Terminal 18. Parking Lot #19 is located between terminals 18 and 19 and is used when the parking lot at Cruise Terminal 18 and the Midport Garage are full. The entrance is on SE 19th Street.

The port authority recommends dropping off luggage and passengers at the terminal before going to park. Try to arrive after 11 a.m. or at least two hours before departure.

Weather

Fort Lauderdale is a tempting place to visit during the summer for its beaches, but summer also is a time of heavier rains than usual.

Rainfall averages eight inches in June, dips in July and climbs again until reaching another high point of eight inches in September.

The dry season goes from November through April, although daytime temperatures drop into the upper 70s Fahrenheit. May is a good month to visit for a combination of warm temperatures and low risk of rain.

Galveston, Texas

Texas is a convenient starting point for a Caribbean cruise for people living in the southwest United States. Galveston is one of two major embarkation ports for the "Friendship" state.

The Port of Galveston is a common starting point for western Caribbean cruises because of the fairly brief distance between it and Cozumel, one of the biggest cruise destinations in the Caribbean. Belize and Roatan, also active cruise destinations, lie just south of Cozumel.

Other destinations for cruises out of Galveston include Jamaica, Grand Cayman, the Bahamas and some eastern Caribbean islands.

Galveston is convenient to reach for people living in Texas and in the western half of the United States. Airline flights from the west coast to Galveston are shorter and less expensive than flights to the major embarkation ports in Florida.

Five ships operate out of the port. Carnival Cruise lines operates three ships and Royal Caribbean and Disney operate one each.

The port has two terminals at 2502 and 2702 Harborside Drive. They are located on Galvest2320n Island, which means travelers will need to take a ferry to reach it. Allow extra time for ferry delays and schedules.

Nearby Attractions

Taking a ferry to reach the Port of Galveston on Galveston Island may require extra time, but the island makes up for it.

Anyone with extra time before or after their cruise will find plenty to do on the island.

The 36-block historic district is located one block from the cruise terminals. It has more than 100 shops, restaurants and galleries in Victorian iron-front buildings, according to the island's Convention and Visitors Bureau.

The island also has the Texas Seaport Museum, Great Storm Theater, 1877 Tall Ship ELISSA, Ocean Star Oil Rig Museum, harbor boat dolphin tours, and the interactive museum Pirates! Legends of the Gulf Coast.

Location and Directions

Two airports serve Galveston and Port of Galveston. They are the George Bush Intercontinental Airport and the Houston Hobby Airport.

The Bush airport is 70 miles northwest of the cruise port and Houston Hobby is 41 miles away.

Carnival offers transfer services between the airport and cruise port that must be scheduled at least five days before going on the cruise.

The transfer rates at the time of this writing were $47 one way and $94 round trip for Bush and $37 one way and $74 round trip for Hobby. See the Carnival Web site for scheduling and more information.

Contact Disney and Royal Caribbean for rates and information on their transfer services. Other commercial companies also offer transfer services. Numerous options are available via online searches.

Drivers from the east will reach to the terminals by taking State Highway 87 West to Galveston Island. They will need to use the Port Bolivar vehicle ferry system to Ferry Road / Highway 87.

Turn right onto Harborside Drive and go 20 blocks. Then take another right onto Kempner / 22nd Street and keep going to the cruise terminal.

Travelers coming from the north and west should take I-45 South to the Galveston Island exit at 1C. Drive on the feeder road to Harborside Drive and turn left.

Go 4.7 miles to Kempner / 22nd Street and turn left. Continue driving until reaching the cruise terminals.

Parking

The Port of Galveston has a $5 discount for prepaid cruise passenger parking. Go to the port Web site at PortOfGalveston.com to reserve a space.

Prepaid parking rates at the time of this writing were $55 for four days, $60 for five days, $70 for six days, $85 for seven days and $90 for eight days. Prices are subject to change. Discounts are available for payment in advance. For more days, contact the port via the Web site's contact links or phone numbers.

Parking can be paid with cash, traveler's checks or Visa, MasterCard or Discover Card credit cards.

Weather

Galveston ranges from slightly warm to slightly hot most of the year. The average high temperatures range from the low 60s Fahrenheit in the winter to the upper 80s in the summer.

Rainfall is moderate with an average of three to four inches a month except September, when it spikes to nearly six inches.

Anyone who likes the weather warm with a low risk of rain should consider going in May through July. But if the cruise is going to the western Caribbean, spring is better because of lower risk of rain on the trip.

Houston, Texas

The Houston Texas cruise port manages to give travelers access to the Caribbean despite the fact that Galveston is a major cruise port only 30 miles away.

Galveston is a popular embarkation point for Caribbean cruises in part because the port is located on Galveston Island in the Gulf of Mexico.

The island is a quicker starting point for a cruise. It also has amenities including a 36-block historic district one block from the cruise terminals. The district has more than 100 shops, restaurants and galleries.

The two ports serve different cruise lines. Galveston caters to customers of Carnival, Disney and Royal Caribbean. Houston serves clients of Princess and Norwegian.

Princess and Norwegian each have one ship that makes Houston its home port. Caribbean Princess and Norwegian Jewel focus on western Caribbean cruises to destinations such as Jamaica, Grand Cayman, Roatan, Cozumel and Belize.

Houston's Bayport Cruise Terminal, 4700 Cruise Road, is actually located in Pasadena on the southeast corner of the Houston city limits. The port has access to Trinity Bay. From there, cruise ships sail past Galveston Island, into the Gulf of Mexico and onward to the Caribbean.

Nearby Attractions

Bush airport is located north of Houston, while Hobby is located south. Cruise travelers who fly into Houston for their trip may want attractions close to their airports.

Ten major attractions in the Houston area are:

- Space Center Houston, 1601 NASA Road 1
- Houston Zoo, 6200 Hermann Park Drive
- Children's Museum of Houston, 1500 Binz St.
- Houston Arboretum and Memorial Park, 4501 Woodway Drive
- The Waterfall and Glenwood Cemetery, 2525 Washington Ave.
- Houston Museum of Natural Science, 5555 Hermann Park Drive
- The Museum of Fine Arts, 1001 Bissonnet St.
- Contemporary Arts Museum Houston, 5216 Montrose Blvd.
- The Rothko and Byzantine Fresco chapels, 3900 Yupon St
- USS Texas (BB-35) and San Jacinto Monument, 3523 Independence Parkway, La Porte

Location and Directions

Two airports serve Bayport Cruise Terminal: William P. Hobby Airport, 22 miles away, and George W. Bush Intercontinental Airport, 45 miles away.

Travel time from Bush Intercontinental is about one hour depending on the time of day. The trip from Hobby Airport may take about 30 minutes.

From the west, take Route 225 east to Route 146 south. Take the Port Road exit and follow the road all the way to the end.

From the south, take I-46 North to the Route 146 north exit. Drive north on 146 to the Port Road exit. Again, follow the road all the way.

Expect to pay $100 to $150 to go from Bush Intercontinental to the terminal by taxi. A one week car rental combined with terminal parking may be a less expensive option.

Parking

The port has 1,500 parking spaces with free on-site shuttles between the lot and the terminal.

The cost is $80 per week or $75 if prepaid. Parking reservations can be made by phone at 877-710-2737 or by going to the port Web site at PortOfHouston.com.

Local Weather

The average high temperature in Houston ranges from 63 degrees Fahrenheit in January to 95 degrees in August, according to historical records from the U.S. National Weather Service.

It rains on average eight to 10 days each month of the year. Total rainfall averages about three inches from December through April and four to five inches the rest of the year.

Jacksonville, Florida

The Jacksonville Florida cruise port may have one of the coolest names of any port that takes travelers on Caribbean cruises.

JaxPort also is the smallest cruise port in Florida after Miami, Fort Lauderdale, Port Canaveral and Tampa.

In fact, it is mainly known as the home port for just one ship, Carnival's Fascination. Fascination goes only to the Bahamas on some trips and the Caribbean on others.

JaxPort is a convenient cruise port for many travelers because Jacksonville is on the northern tip of Florida's east coast. Its location is much closer for drivers from the north than other Florida cruise ports. JaxPort is 353 miles north of Miami's port.

Nearby Attractions

Travelers who use the above directions will see that Zoo Parkway is a common route to the cruise terminal. It is named Zoo Parkway because it also leads to one of Jacksonville's biggest attractions -- and one of the closest to the cruise terminal. Jacksonville Zoo and Gardens, 370 Zoo Parkway, has 2,000 animals and 1,000 varieties of plants.

Cruise travelers with more time on their hands will find that Jacksonville's beaches are the biggest attraction in the area. The city has more than 20 miles of them. Jacksonville Beach, Neptune Beach and Ponte Vedra Beach are a 30-minute drive southeast of the terminal.

The Jacksonville Museum of Science and Industry, which was formerly the Jacksonville Children's Museum, has a planetarium, seven permanent exhibits and various temporary exhibits. Also known as MOSH, the museum is at 1025 Museum Circle or about 13 miles southwest of the cruise terminal.

Jacksonville Landing on the St. John's River in downtown Jacksonville is a waterfront shopping, dining and entertainment district. The district, which offers about 350 events every year, is located on Independence Drive about 12 miles southwest of the cruise terminal and near the MOSH museum.

The city's Riverside Avondale Neighborhood has more than 5,000 historical buildings, an arts market and an art museum. It is located at the southwestern edge of Jacksonville.

Location and Directions

JaxPort is at 9810 August Drive near the northwest corner of Dames Point. It is bordered by Heckscher Drive and I-295.

Visitors coming from the north should take I-95 south to the I-295 south exit. Go on I-295 for six miles and get off at exit 41. Turn right onto Zoo Parkway, cross New Berlin Road, go about a half mile and turn left into the cruise terminal entrance.

Visitors coming from the south should take I-95 north to exit 337, merge onto I-95 north and go 18 miles. Take exit 41 and turn left onto Zoo Parkway. Cross New Berlin Road, go about a half mile and turn left into the terminal entrance.

Jacksonville International Airport is located 12 miles to the northwest of JaxPort. The airport doesn't have rental car companies on the property, but several are located nearby. The cruise port has franchised taxi and shuttle service that transfer passengers from the airport.

Parking

The parking lot opens at 10:30 a.m. on cruise days. Reservations are not required. Travelers can pay with cash or credit card on site or go to the JaxPort Web site at jaxport.com to pay in advance.

Parking costs $17 per day per vehicle and $34 a day for oversized vehicles that require two spaces.

Local Weather

Jacksonville is in Florida, but that doesn't mean warm temperatures year round. It is the northernmost Florida cruise port, so winters are a bit cool.

Average daytime temperatures range between the mid 60s Fahrenheit during the winter to the high 80s in the summer, according to the U.S. National Weather Service.

Like the rest of Florida, it has a distinct dry season from November to May with average rainfall of about three inches a month. The rainy season goes from June through October with average rainfall of about six to seven inches a month.

Miami, Florida

The Miami cruise port has often been named the busiest in the world thanks to its convenient location.

This major city on the east coast of Florida has easy access to both the Bahama islands and the entire Caribbean.

Visitors from the U.S., Canada and Europe often fly into the Miami International Airport and take a quick taxi over to the cruise terminals. They are only eight miles away.

PortMiami, also known as the Port of Miami, has seven terminals. We were pleasantly surprised at how quickly we reached the port in such a big city after landing at the airport. It is worth noting that rush hour may slow the traffic time.

Nearby Attractions

Visitors who arrive early enough or stay overnight may have a chance to take advantage of nearby tourist attractions.

Miami Beach is the best known beach in the area. It is 13 miles or about 23 minutes by car from the airport.

Cultural attractions in the city of Miami include Adrienne Arsht Center for the Performing Arts, 1300 Biscayne Boulevard; HistoryMiami, a city history museum at 101 W Flagler Street; and Miami Art Museum, 1103 Biscayne Boulevard.

Bayside is a dining, shopping and entertainment district at R106, 401 Biscayne Boulevard. Families may have an interest in the Miami Children's Museum, 980 MacArthur Causeway, or the Jungle Island nature preserve, 1111 Parrot Jungle Trail.

Outdoor enthusiasts can visit various attractions near the Everglades along Route 41 including the Everglades Safari Park, which is 26 miles or about 35 minutes by car. Miccosukee Indian Village and Mitchell Landing Big Cypress National Preserve lie just to the west of it.

Anyone with a little more time and a rental car can take a 55-minute ride south to Everglades National Park. Ernest F. Coe Visitor Center is the closest visitor center.

Finally, people with even more time on their hands can take Route 1 south to the Florida Keys. The largest and closest key is Key Largo, which is 63 miles or an hour and 15 minutes.

Location and Directions

The address for PortMiami is 1015 North America Way, Miami, Florida, 33132.

Visitors who drive will find that major highways have direct access to the Port Miami Tunnel that leads into the port:

Anyone taking I-95 south toward Miami should take the eastbound I-395 ramp at Miami Beach. Keep going on I-395 East until reaching the tunnel entrance on the left.

People taking I-95 north toward Miami should go to the Eastbound I-395 ramp at Miami Beach. Continue on I-395 East and the MacArthur Causeway and stay alert for signs signaling the tunnel entrance on the left.

Visitors driving from the south should go on SR-826 North to SR-836 East, then head east on SR-836 to I-395 East (Miami Beach). Keep going on I-395 East/MacArthur Causeway and until reaching the tunnel entrance on the left.

People who arrive by taxi, limousine or shuttle bus will be able to get out in front of their terminal. Drive-in passengers can park at the port.

Parking

Taxis that go from the airport to the cruise terminals have a flat rate of $24. For overnight parking, plan to pay $22 per night.

Note that these prices are subject to change. The garages take major credit cards, but they do not accept debit cards.

Another option for visitors is the Metrorail Orange Line. It goes from the airport to the terminals in about a half hour.

Local Weather

Miami is one of the southernmost cities in the United States, so it gladly gives cruise visitors plenty of warm weather for most of the year. But it's not always beach weather.

Average daytime temperatures range from the mid 70s Fahrenheit in the winter to the upper 80s in the summer.

But the summer also is the rainy season. It goes from May through October and brings up to eight inches of rain a month during some months. The dry season from November through April averages only two to three inches a month.

Mobile, Alabama

Mobile Alabama has taken on its own role as a Caribbean cruise port in partnership with Carnival Cruise Lines.

All cruises out of Mobile go to the western Caribbean on Carnival Fantasy. They are mostly four and five day cruises to Cozumel and Yucatan throughout the year (at the time of this writing).

Nearby Attractions

The USS Alabama Battleship Memorial Park, 2703 Battleship Parkway, is three miles east of the cruise terminal off I-10. Cruise passengers coming to the terminal from the east will find that visiting the park will be convenient before or after the cruise.

Visitors will be able to explore the battleship along with the submarine USS Drum as well as an aircraft collection. Tickets are $15 for anyone 12 and older, $6 for children 6-11 and free for children under 6. Discounts are available for senior citizens and military personnel.

Anyone with less time should note that the cruise terminal is next to Cooper Riverside Park. The park is home to GulfQuest National Maritime Museum of the Gulf of Mexico. The museum has 90 interactive exhibits and theaters in a building designed like a container ship. It offers displays about marine archeology, shipwrecks, hurricanes, shipbuilding and other maritime topics.

Tickets are $18 for adults 18 and older, $16 for teens and $14 for children 5-12. The museum is open from Tuesday through Sunday and closed on Mondays.

Anyone with a limited budget, limited time and an interest in history will find that Fort Conde, 150 South Royal Street, will serve all three goals. This re-creation of the original fort built in the early 18th century is free to the public and located within walking distance of both the terminal and the GulfQuest museum.

Visitors will see interactive exhibits and artifacts of the original settlers of Mobile. The museum is open from 8:30 a.m. to 4:30 p.m. daily.

Location and Directions

Mobile Cruise Terminal, 201 S. Water St., is located in downtown Mobile a half mile from I-10 and six miles from the junction of I-10 and I-65. More than a half dozen hotels are located within a brief drive of the terminal.

From I-65 south, stay on I-65 southbound until it meets I-10. Take I-10 east to exit 26A at Canal Street. Turn right after the exit ramp onto Water Street. Stay on Water Street for two blocks. The garage and terminal are on the right.

From I-10 west, go across the Mobile Bayway bridge and through the I-10 George Wallace Tunnel. Take exit 25A at Texas Street and follow the signs back onto I-10 East. Stay in the right lane and take exit 26A at Canal Street. Turn right at the end of the ramp onto Water Street. Stay on Water Street for two blocks. The garage and terminal are on the right side.

From I-10 east, stay eastbound almost to downtown Mobile. Take exit 26A at Canal Street. Turn right at the end of the ramp onto Water Street. Stay on Water Street for two blocks. The garage and terminal are on the right side.

Parking

To reach the Alabama Cruise Terminal parking lot, turn right on Eslava Street and follow directions by an attendant or police officer into the garage.

A terminal employee will unload, tag and transfer luggage. Passengers should go to the garage ramp to pay for parking. The fee for regular-sized cars is $18 a day. The fee for RVs and campers if $144 for four days, $180 for five days and $252 for seven days. Fees are subject to change without notice.

Visitors should park the car and walk to the glass doors at the garage's north end. Take the stairs or elevator to the lobby and show documentation to the terminal employees, who will show where to go to the check-in and screening areas.

If the parking lot is full, attendants will direct passengers to off-site parking and will return on a terminal shuttle.

Local Weather

Despite its far south location, Mobile is cooler and wetter than Florida cruise ports, especially during the winter. But it's also more convenient for people living in the western half of the United States and Canada.

Average daytime temperatures range from about 60 degrees Fahrenheit in the winter to nearly 90 in the summer. Rainfall is consistently moderate to slightly heavy with an average of four to seven inches a month.

New Orleans, Louisiana

The New Orleans cruise port is a starting point for many western Caribbean cruises.

It is the sixth largest cruise port in the United States because of its convenient location to that region of the Caribbean.

Officially called Port of New Orleans, the facility is home to ships from Royal Caribbean, Carnival Cruise Line and Norwegian Cruise Line. Ships dock at two nearby terminals at New Orleans Place.

Nearby Attractions

Anyone wanting to spend even a small amount of time in New Orleans before or after their cruise will find quick access to major attractions.

The terminals are located in the heart of downtown within walking distance of the French Quarter and Bourbon Street, the city's most famous attraction. This National Historic Landmark is known for its cobblestone streets, restaurants, nightclubs and carriage tours.

Another nearby attraction is the World War II Museum at 945 Magazine Street. It is about one mile northwest of the port.

Visitors with less time on their hands may hop on the Riverfront trolley line next to the port. It goes one and a half miles past the French Market to the Aquarium of the Americas, shopping at the Riverwalk and the Morial convention center.

The Riverwalk Marketplace and Outlet Collection at Riverwalk are two shopping and dining centers even closer to the port. They can be found within a brief walking distance north of the terminals.

Location and Directions

The port has two terminals for cruise passengers. They are the Julia Street Cruise Terminal Complex and the Erato Street Cruise Terminal Complex.

The Julia Street Cruise terminal, 920 Port of New Orleans Place, is the location for Norwegian and Royal Caribbean ships.

It is between the Erato Street Cruise Terminal Complex and The Outlet Collection at Riverwalk.

The Erato Street Cruise terminal, 1100 Port of New Orleans Place, accommodates ships from Carnival.

Anyone flying into New Orleans to reach the cruise terminals will likely land at The Louis Armstrong International Airport. It is 17 miles or about 45 minutes from the cruise terminals depending on traffic volume and time of day.

Visitors can use an airport shuttle, airport limousine or taxi to reach the terminals from the airport. Expect to pay $20+ for the shuttle, $58+ for a limousine and $35+ for a taxi at the time of this writing and depending on the number of travelers.

Anyone driving to the terminals will take I-10 east to New Orleans and the N.O. Business District, US90 West, Crescent City Connection to the West Bank. Take exit 11C, go right onto Tchoupitoulas Street and left onto Henderson Street. Pass the railroad tracks and turn left onto Port of New Orleans Place.

Parking

It has more than 1,000 parking spaces on top of the terminal with luggage assistance. An elevator goes to the embarkation deck.

Parking is available for cars at $20 a day; recreational vehicles pay about twice as much. Prices are subject to change. Reservations are not required except for oversized vehicles. Visitors should have their cruise tickets available to gain access to the parking lots.

The nearest available parking that is not on site is four blocks away, according to the Port of New Orleans Web site.

Local Weather

The average high temperatures in New Orleans range from about 60 degrees Fahrenheit in January to 90 degrees during the summer.

Rainfall averages between four and six inches a month except for three inches in October, according to the U.S. National Weather Service.

Port Canaveral (Orlando), Florida

Families with a large enough budget may combine a world-famous amusement park and a Caribbean cruise thanks to Port Canaveral.

Port Canaveral is named after the Cape Canaveral Air Force Station, which is the location of early space launches.

The port is an active embarkation point for cruise lines including Carnival, Disney, Norwegian and Royal Caribbean. It is on the east coast of Florida about midway between Jacksonville to the north and Miami to the south.

Nearby Attractions

Port Canaveral is just one hour east of Orlando's Disney World and Universal Studios.

Families who don't have the time or budget to combine a cruise with an amusement park may instead want to visit another world-famous attraction. The Kennedy Space Center and shuttle landing facility are 17 miles north of Port Canaveral on Merritt Island.

The port lies on a thin strip of land that includes the city of Cocoa Beach. Attractions include the beach itself as well as the well-known Cocoa Beach Pier and several parks.

The beach and pier are only three and a half miles from the port, so visitors with a little extra time can hit the beach before or after their cruise.

Location and Directions

Anyone driving to the port from the north or south can take I-95 to 528 / A1A east. The distance from the exit to the port is about 13 miles.

The port has eight active terminals. The city and zip codes for each are Cape Canaveral and 32920.

Cruise Terminal #1 - 9050 Discovery Road
Cruise Terminal #2 - 180 Christopher Columbus Drive
Cruise Terminal #3 - 220 Christopher Columbus Drive
Cruise Terminal #4 - 240 Christopher Columbus Drive

Cruise Terminal #5 - 9245 Charles Rowland Drive
Cruise Terminal #6 - 9241 Charles Rowland Drive
Cruise Terminal #8 - 9155 Charles Rowland Drive
Cruise Terminal #10 - 9005 Charles Rowland Drive

Orlando Sanford International Airport is the largest airport serving the port. Others include Melbourne International Airport, Space Coast Regional Airport and Daytona Beach International Airport.

Melbourne is the closest airport at 25 miles away. Orlando is 45 miles away but easily accessible using the Route 528 / Martin Andersen Beachline Expressway.

Anyone who wants to spend time on Florida beaches before or after their cruise may want to land at Daytona Beach International Airport. It is about one hour or 72 miles north of Port Canaveral.

Parking

Visitors can pay for parking at the cruise terminals with cash, Mastercard, Visa or traveler's checks.

Parking prices are $17 per day for both cars and RVs. Prices are subject to change.

The port Web site has the ability to schedule parking in advance based on the cruise ship, cruise length and departure date.

Discounts are available for guests staying at a select list of nearby hotels. Check with the hotel for details on the discount.
For more information, go to the Port Canaveral Web site: http://www.portcanaveral.com/

Local Weather

The June through September rainy season hits Orlando and Port Canaveral especially hard. The area has an average rainfall of six to eight inches a month for all four months.

The rest of the year is much better with an average of two to three inches a month. Beach lovers in particular might want to go in May, which has the best historical average for a combination of warmth and low risk of rain.

Average daytime temperatures range from about 70 degrees Fahrenheit in the winter to 90 in the summer.

Tampa, Florida

Tampa is a rising player in cruise embarkation ports for the Caribbean because of its nearby airport, major attractions and the development of Port Tampa Bay.

It also has become the home port for ships from Carnival Cruise Lines, Holland America, Royal Caribbean and Norwegian Cruise Line.

Nearby Attractions

Visitors who plan to leave from Tampa and return there on a cruise will find a major shopping, dining and entertainment venue at Channelside. Entertainment options include an IMAX theater, the Florida Aquarium and an outdoor plaza with concerts.

Busch Gardens Tampa, 10165 N Malcolm McKinley Drive, is a 335-acre theme park with rides, shows, roller coasters and animal encounters. Other major attractions in the city include Florida Aquarium, Glazer

Children's Museum and Tampa Museum of Art.

Good beaches require a little driving because Tampa the city is tucked inside Tampa Bay.

Clearwater Beach, about 40 minutes west of the cruise docks, is an easy and popular choice. Caladesi Island State Park is just north of Clearwater Beach and takes 50 minutes to get there.

The closest beach to the cruise docks is Ben T. Davis Beach, about 25 minutes away on Old Tampa Bay. Route 60 going west from the docks will take visitors to Davis Beach and onward to Clearwater Beach if Davis isn't appealing enough.

Location and Directions

The port has three terminals numbered 2, 3 and 6. Carnival docks at Terminal 2, 651 Channelside Drive; Norwegian and Royal Caribbean dock at Terminal 3, 815 Channelside Drive; and Holland America docks at Terminal 6, 1333 McKay Street. The zip code for each is 33602.

Port Tampa Bay is located nine miles from Tampa International Airport, which makes it a quick ride via taxi or rental car

Some visitors may land at Orlando International Airport if they find the flights there are less expensive or if they plan to spend time at Universal Studios or Disney World. The distance from the airport to the cruise terminal is 86 miles.

Orlando drivers should take I-4 west to exit 1. Go south on 21st Street, right on Adamo Drive / Highway 60 then left onto Channelside Drive.

Visitors taking I-275 should go on I-4 east to exit 1. Travel south on 21st

Street, right on Adamo Drive (Hwy 60) and left onto Channelside Drive.

From the Tampa airport, follow the signs to I-275 North, which will merge with I-4 East. Travel on I-4 East to Exit 1, go south on 21st Street and turn right on Adamo Drive (Highway 60). Take a left onto Channelside Drive.

Parking

Parking is located across the street from Terminals 2 and 3 and adjacent to Terminal 6. It offers both valet parking and self-service parking.

The port Web site at tampaport.com provides a link for visitors to pre-pay for their parking.

Parking prices average about $15 a day for cars. Expect to pay about double the rate for oversized parking. Valet parking costs about $20 more. Prices are subject to change.

Local Weather

Tampa suffers from the same heavy rains during the summer as the rest of the Caribbean.

Average rainfall historically peaks during the rainy season from June through September according to the U.S. National Weather Service. August is the worst month with an average of seven inches.

The dry season goes from October through May with an average of about two to three inches of rain per month.

Average high temperatures range from 70 degrees Fahrenheit or 21 Celsius in January to 90 Fahrenheit or 32 Celsius during the summer months.